The Celts: A Very Short Introduction

VERY SHORT INTRODUCTIONS are for anyone wanting a stimulating and accessible way in to a new subject. They are written by experts, and have been published in more than 25 languages worldwide.

The series began in 1995, and now represents a wide variety of topics in history, philosophy, religion, science, and the humanities. Over the next few years it will grow to a library of around 200 volumes – a Very Short Introduction to everything from ancient Egypt and Indian philosophy to conceptual art and cosmology.

Very Short Introductions available now:

ANCIENT PHILOSOPHY
  Julia Annas
THE ANGLO-SAXON AGE
  John Blair
ANIMAL RIGHTS   David DeGrazia
ARCHAEOLOGY   Paul Bahn
ARCHITECTURE
  Andrew Ballantyne
ARISTOTLE   Jonathan Barnes
ART HISTORY   Dana Arnold
ART THEORY   Cynthia Freeland
THE HISTORY OF
  ASTRONOMY   Michael Hoskin
ATHEISM   Julian Baggini
AUGUSTINE   Henry Chadwick
BARTHES   Jonathan Culler
THE BIBLE   John Riches
BRITISH POLITICS
  Anthony Wright
BUDDHA   Michael Carrithers
BUDDHISM   Damien Keown
CAPITALISM   James Fulcher
THE CELTS   Barry Cunliffe
CHOICE THEORY
  Michael Allingham
CHRISTIAN ART   Beth Williamson
CLASSICS   Mary Beard and
  John Henderson
CLAUSEWITZ   Michael Howard
THE COLD WAR
  Robert McMahon

CONTINENTAL PHILOSOPHY
  Simon Critchley
COSMOLOGY   Peter Coles
CRYPTOGRAPHY
  Fred Piper and Sean Murphy
DADA AND SURREALISM
  David Hopkins
DARWIN   Jonathan Howard
DEMOCRACY   Bernard Crick
DESCARTES   Tom Sorell
DRUGS   Leslie Iversen
THE EARTH   Martin Redfern
EGYPTIAN MYTHOLOGY
  Geraldine Pinch
EIGHTEENTH-CENTURY
  BRITAIN   Paul Langford
THE ELEMENTS   Philip Ball
EMOTION   Dylan Evans
EMPIRE   Stephen Howe
ENGELS   Terrell Carver
ETHICS   Simon Blackburn
THE EUROPEAN UNION
  John Pinder
EVOLUTION
  Brian and Deborah Charlesworth
FASCISM   Kevin Passmore
THE FRENCH REVOLUTION
  William Doyle
FREUD   Anthony Storr
GALILEO   Stillman Drake
GANDHI   Bhikhu Parekh

Available soon:

AFRICAN HISTORY
  John Parker and Richard Rathbone
ANCIENT EGYPT   Ian Shaw
THE BRAIN   Michael O'Shea
BUDDHIST ETHICS
  Damien Keown
CHAOS   Leonard Smith
CHRISTIANITY   Linda Woodhead
CITIZENSHIP   Richard Bellamy
CLASSICAL ARCHITECTURE
  Robert Tavernor
CLONING   Arlene Judith Klotzko
CONTEMPORARY ART
  Julian Stallabrass
THE CRUSADES
  Christopher Tyerman
DERRIDA   Simon Glendinning
DESIGN   John Heskett
DINOSAURS   David Norman
DREAMING   J. Allan Hobson
ECONOMICS   Partha Dasgupta
THE END OF THE WORLD
  Bill McGuire
EXISTENTIALISM   Thomas Flynn
THE FIRST WORLD WAR
  Michael Howard
FREE WILL   Thomas Pink
FUNDAMENTALISM
  Malise Ruthven
HABERMAS   Gordon Finlayson

HIEROGLYPHS
  Penelope Wilson
HIROSHIMA   B. R. Tomlinson
HUMAN EVOLUTION
  Bernard Wood
INTERNATIONAL RELATIONS
  Paul Wilkinson
JAZZ   Brian Morton
MANDELA   Tom Lodge
MEDICAL ETHICS
  Tony Hope
THE MIND   Martin Davies
MYTH   Robert Segal
NATIONALISM   Steven Grosby
PERCEPTION   Richard Gregory
PHILOSOPHY OF RELIGION
  Jack Copeland and Diane Proudfoot
PHOTOGRAPHY
  Steve Edwards
THE RAJ   Denis Judd
THE RENAISSANCE
  Jerry Brotton
RENAISSANCE ART
  Geraldine Johnson
SARTRE   Christina Howells
THE SPANISH CIVIL WAR
  Helen Graham
TRAGEDY   Adrian Poole
THE TWENTIETH CENTURY
  Martin Conway

For more information visit our web site
www.oup.co.uk/vsi

Barry Cunliffe

THE CELTS

A Very Short Introduction

OXFORD
UNIVERSITY PRESS

OXFORD

UNIVERSITY PRESS

Great Clarendon Street, Oxford OX2 6DP

Oxford University Press is a department of the University of Oxford.
It furthers the University's objective of excellence in research, scholarship,
and education by publishing worldwide in

Oxford New York

Auckland Bangkok Buenos Aires Cape Town Chennai
Dar es Salaam Delhi Hong Kong Istanbul Karachi Kolkata
Kuala Lumpur Madrid Melbourne Mexico City Mumbai Nairobi
São Paulo Shanghai Taipei Tokyo Toronto

Oxford is a registered trade mark of Oxford University Press
in the UK and in certain other countries

Published in the United States
by Oxford University Press Inc., New York

British Library Cataloguing in Publication Data

Data available

Library of Congress Cataloging in Publication Data

Data available

ISBN 978-0-19-280418-1

7 9 10 8 6

Typeset by RefineCatch Ltd, Bungay, Suffolk
Printed in Italy by
Legoprint S.p.A., Lavis (TN)

Contents

List of illustrations

Chapter 1
All things to all men

Some years ago, after writing a book, *The Celtic World*, I received a letter from an American. He was, he said, an alcoholic and it had worried him but having read of the Celtic love of wine – a story told by the Classical writer Athenaeus of the Gauls – he was much reassured. His grandparents had been Celts from Scotland and his behaviour was thus explained: it was part of his Celticness and he would henceforth be proud of it. Many reading this might find it an innocuous story, and might indeed gain some reassurance for their own occasional overindulgences, but others might become apoplectic seeing in it yet further evidence of the insidious Celtic myth perpetuated by popular books. One academic member of this camp has even gone so far as to suggest that some authors deliberately use the word 'Celtic' in book titles to boost sales. Could there be something in this? I have before me a glossy flyer from a book club inviting members to join 'A Celtic Odyssey' embracing 'The Beauty and Wonder of a Lost Civilization' and to choose from a range of conflations with such alluring titles as *Celtic Wisdom Tarot Pack*, *Spiritual Wisdom from the Celtic World*, *The Celtic Tree Oracle*, and *Celtic Body Decoration Kit*. Should you wish to indulge the odyssey still further your local shops might offer Celtic jewellery or instructions for creating Celtic knotwork. And try the telephone directory, particularly in Atlantic-facing parts of the British Isles, to see how many commercial enterprises offer 'Celtic' services. Celts are well and truly embedded in our everyday life – at least in popular perception.

But there are other levels to this. Music, for example, is undergoing a Celtic renaissance, nowhere more impressive than in the *Festival Interceltic de Lorient*, heir to the Bagpipes Festival that was held at Brest from 1953 to 1970. Here international groups, including The Chieftains and Gaelic Storm, play to the same audiences as Breton stars like Alan Stivell. Denez Prigent's report in *Carn* of the 2001 Festival claimed attendances of 500,000: 'going beyond the "folkloric" it has opened Breton music to the ocean winds and invited to its celebration all the scattered members of the great Celtic family'. At a less pop level, the compositions and performances of the Breton pianist Didier Squiben, blending the cadences and rhythms of traditional folk music with echoes of the wind and the sea, provide a vivid example of the vitality of modern music in its Celtic guise.

'Celtic' cultural events may also sometimes play to political and economic agendas. In Venice, in 1991, under the auspices of the Palazzo Grassi, a spectacular exhibition of Iron Age artefacts, brought together from all over Europe, opened under the title 'The Celts, the Origins of Europe'. The event was sponsored by Fiat. In a curiously muddled introduction, published in the lavish exhibition catalogue, the President of Palazzo Grassi explained

> This exhibition is a tribute both to the new Europe which cannot come into fruition without a comprehensive awareness of its unity, and to the fact that, in addition to its Roman and Christian sources, today's Europe traces its roots from its Celtic heritage which is there for all to see.

Here some vague concept of 'Celtic heritage' seems to be being drawn into the service of the ideal of European Union. Is Celticness in this context being used simply as a metaphor or is there somewhere lurking behind this an unspoken belief in a Celtic race and a long-gone heroic age?

'Our common Celtic heritage' has been, and no doubt will continue to be, the rallying call for many political movements. In 1867, at a time when Bretons were desperately trying to preserve their language and traditions against the cultural imperialism of the centralized French state, Hersart de La Villemarqué, author of the famous *Barzaz-Breiz* (*Songs of Brittany*), sent out a call for what was to become the first Interceltic Congress, to be held at Saint-Brieuc. His appeal was to his 'compatriots from Wales, brothers from Cornwall and cousins from Ireland and Scotland'. In 2001 the Interceltic Congress, held at Rennes, was attended by 200 delegates, half from Brittany and the other half from 'other Celtic countries'. The theme of the conference was 'History in the Celtic Countries Nowadays – People without memory are people with no future'.

The Venice exhibition and the Rennes Congress ten years later, both predicated on the concept of Celt, were proclaiming very different messages. At Venice, Celticness was a motif used to underpin the belief in a unified Europe, while at Rennes it provided identity and strength for communities living along the Atlantic façade against what they perceived to be the threat of the centralizing tendencies of European states, particularly the governments based in London, Paris, and Madrid. Who is right? Is anyone right, or wrong, for that matter? Or should we accept, as J. R. R. Tolkien wrote in 1963, that 'anything is possible in the fabulous Celtic twilight, which is not so much a twilight of the gods as of the reason', remembering, as the great Celtic scholar David Ellis Evans sternly pointed out in 1999, that Tolkien's aside was meant specifically to make fun of certain extreme linguistic entomologies and not to be all embracing.

So from New Age body decoration to concerns for the survival of regional identity, from half-baked attempts at political manipulation to an inspiration for new music, the Celtic spectre hovers while the Celtic sceptre is held aloft. Celticness does indeed seem to be all things to all men. Perhaps, as Simon James claimed in his 1999 book *The Atlantic Celts Ancient People or Modern Invention*, 'Celticism . . . has, in many respects, long been a complacent orthodoxy ripe for re-evaluation'.

There have, in the last decade or so, been a number of voices, mostly of archaeologists, raised against current usages of the word Celt. Some are voices of reason, asking for greater critical rigour to be exercised, others adopt a more strident note. One of the more vociferous critics is John Collis who, in 'States without Centres', complains that Celtic society described by some modern authors

> merely represents a mishmash of information from different times and different places which is often of little value for understanding the societies being described. Descriptions, or rather caricature, of societies cannot be transposed in time and space under an invented concept of the 'Celts'; indeed the whole use of the terms Celt and Celtic is something which should be avoided as it distorts our understanding of the archaeological record.

In his contribution to *Los Celtas en Europa* he warns of 'modern politicised utilisation of the concept of "Celts"' and goes on to claim that 'archaeologists have a duty to inform the general public of the hidden agenda behind this modern use of the "Celts"'. There are two different but related concerns here, the first focusing largely on the way that ancient Celts have been characterized and presented, the second on concepts of modern Celticity. Both are legitimate areas for debate.

The second of these concerns was taken up by Simon James in *The Atlantic Celts*. The essence of James's argument lies in his assertion that 'The Ancient Celts of Britain and Ireland are an essentially bogus and recent invention'. His book contained little with which an archaeologist or historian would have been unfamiliar, but his opinions, offered in public before publication, appeared to be shockingly new and were presented by some journalists as an outrageous attack on devolution. The *Daily Telegraph* of 12 March 1998 reported that certain archaeologists had 'angered self-proclaimed Celts from Scotland to Cornwall by their claims that the Celtic culture, much trumpeted during the weeks before devolution referendums in Wales and Scotland, is historical "fantasy"'. Many feathers were, understandably, ruffled.

In more sober mood James lays out his stall in his first chapter with two basic claims: 'no one in Britain or Ireland called themselves a "Celt" or "Celtic" before 1700' and 'The Welsh, Scots, Irish and other peoples have only come to describe themselves and their ancestors as Celts since the eighteenth century. The notion of insular Celts, past and present, then is a modern interpretation and an adopted "ethnonym"'. With the small, but not unimportant, proviso that the first contention should have read 'no one in Britain or Ireland *is recorded to have* called themselves a "Celt" or "Celtic" before 1700', these two basic statements are a fair reflection of the situation. The rest of his book substantiates them and explores how the widely accepted concept of the Celtic West has come into being.

What all this means, of course, is that the widely asked questions – when did the Celts arrive in Britain and where did they come from? – become somewhat redundant. But how is it that the belief in one or more Celtic invasions into these islands first came about? Some of the details we will return to later, but the short answer is that the idea really took off after the antiquarian scholar Edward Lhuyd coined the word Celtic for a group of languages – Irish, Welsh, Cornish, and Breton – and published an account of them and their similarities in his great work *Archaeologia Britannica* in 1707. He noted that a close relationship existed between Gaulish, Irish, and British and also between Welsh, Cornish, and Breton and then went on to impose a historical interpretation on these two groups (Q-Celtic and P-Celtic as they later became known). First, he suggested, Irish Britons moved from Gaul to settle in the British Isles but then were later pushed into northern Britain and Ireland by a second wave of Gauls who settled in the south and west.

This early eighteenth-century hypothesis has driven the debate ever since. Its longevity is truly remarkable and due in no small part to the fact that linguists and archaeologists were for a long time prepared to accept each other's interpretations, each gaining reassurance by building upon the other in an uncritical circle of mutually supporting assertion lacking firm foundation. One wonders how many other early eighteenth-century hypotheses have set the scientific agenda for nearly two centuries!

So it was that, almost by accident and default, the inhabitants of the British Isles and Ireland came to be known as Celtic. When Sir Augustus Wollaston Franks, a Keeper at the British Museum, produced a catalogue of British decorated metalwork in 1863, he chose the term 'Late Keltic' to describe items of Iron Age date. The phrase was used throughout the first edition of the *British Museum Guide to the Antiquities of the Early Iron Age* (1905), but by the time of the second edition (1925) the characterization was dropped because, as the preface cautiously noted, 'There is some uncertainty as to the existence or date of an earlier Keltic civilization in these islands.' The cracks in the hypothesis were beginning to appear, but only now, seventy years on, have the sledgehammers of the archaeologists begun to batter the already-fractured edifice in earnest.

At the beginning of the twenty-first century the Celtic debate is in full flood, with all shades of opinion being expressed – in the title of a 1998 article by Patrick Sims Williams – "from celtomania to celtoscepticism." The debate is lively and sometimes a little bad-tempered, but what all contestants will agree on is the intriguing complexity of the subject. There are many strands of very disparate data to be examined. The direct archaeological evidence contributes insights into ritual behaviour, burial practices, settlement layouts, and a wide array of material culture including distinctive art styles commonly referred to as Celtic Art. Linguistic studies show something of the extent, development and survival of the group of closely related languages which, after Lhuyd, we still call Celtic. Then there are the Classical sources – Greek and Roman writers with their references to *Celti*, *Celtae*, *Keltoi*, *Celtici*, *Galli*, *Gallici*, and *Galatae* – curious barbarians to be caricatured and used as local colour in the many 'histories' presenting the interactions and conflicts from which the Graeco-Roman world would, through the craft of the writer, emerge triumphant.

Nor can we overlook the potential contribution of the rich vernacular literature of Ireland and Wales and the ancient Law tracts of these countries – texts built up from ancient oral traditions modified over generations and layered with accretions at each retelling.

It is a rich mix of ingredients, but what we cannot do is to fling them all into one pot and expect a perfectly formed Celt to emerge. Each of the different categories of evidence has to be considered within its own critical parameters to separate fact from wishful thinking and to distil out what it has to offer to the debate. Whether, in this process of deconstruction, Celts and Celticism will vanish altogether remains to be seen. To find out, read on.

Chapter 2
A view from the Mediterranean

'If the heavens and earth are divided into four parts, the Indians will occupy the land of the east wind, the Ethiopians the regions from which the south wind blows, the Celts the west, and the Scythians the land of the north wind.' This was the world view of Greek historian Ephorus of Cymae, whose great work *Universal History*, in thirty books, was written in the first half of the fourth century BC. The original text has long since disappeared but this particular scrap survives as a quotation in Strabo's *Geography* (1.2.28), compiled nearly three centuries later. Ephorus' understanding of the world was that of any educated Greek – Europe was occupied by two principal peoples: the Scythians in the east, living around the north and west shores of the Black Sea and extending, perhaps, into the Middle Danube region – what is now the Great Hungarian Plain – and the Celts to the west of them. Elsewhere Strabo tells us that Ephorus believed *Celtica* to be so large that it included most of Iberia as far as Gades (Cadiz). In this he was probably following Herodotus of Halicarnassus, who wrote his *History* in the fifth century. For him the Celts lived beyond the Pillars of Hercules (the Straits of Gibraltar) bordering on the Cynesii, who were the westernmost inhabitants of Europe occupying what is now southern Portugal.

Herodotus also offers other tantalizing scraps of Celtic geography. He tells us that the Danube rose in the land of the Celts near the city of Pyrene. If Pyrene refers to the Pyrenees, then he is probably scrambling together different pieces of information he has learned of the Celts, that the Danube rose in Celtic lands and that the Celts lived near the Pyrenees.

An even earlier source is the ethnographer Hecataeus of Miletus, who was about in the late sixth century BC. From scraps of his lost work quoted by others we learn that Narbon (near modern Narbonne in southern France) was a Celtic city and trading centre and that Massalia (Marseilles) was a Greek city founded in Ligurian territory near Celtica. He also lists Nyrax as a Celtic city but its location is unknown, though some argue that it may have been Noricum in Austria.

It is not much to go on. At best it suggests that the early Greek geographers had only a vague idea of European geography and were content to lump together most of the barbarians of Europe from the Middle Danube to the Atlantic as Celts, while recognizing that there were others within this region who were not Celts.

But what of the name, *Keltoi*? Is it a general-purpose term dreamed up by the Greeks to refer collectively to the disparate northern barbarians they encountered (rather like Eskimo was used to describe the peoples of the circumpolar zone in more recent times)? Some light on this is thrown by Julius Caesar. Writing of Gaul (France) in the mid-first century BC he states, quite deliberately of the inhabitants, presumably in an attempt at clarification, 'we call [them] Gauls though in their own language they are called Celts'. Writing two centuries later, the Greek Pausanius emphasizes that *Keltoi* was a far more ancient name than *Galli*. Other writers use the terms *Keltoi/Celtae* and *Galli/Galatae* as though they are interchangeable.

So where does all this leave us? The simplest interpretation is that there were specific peoples who, from at least as early as the sixth century BC, called themselves Celts, and that in Caesar's time they occupied central Gaul roughly between the Gironde and the Seine. The term *Galli/Galatae*, which may mean 'stranger' or 'enemy', is more likely to be a general-purpose name by which northern barbarians, among them the Celts, were referred to by others. Whether all *Galli/Galatae* regarded themselves as Celts is completely unknown. At first sight it looks as though the Classical writers are being sloppy in their usage, but in reality it may be a reflection of a very fluid situation in temperate Europe with different tribes coming together in confederations and allegiances and adopting the names of the more pre-eminent. In the fourth century BC when there appears to have been increased mobility, including major folk movements (see Chapter 5), it is likely that small groups from different tribes coalesced into larger movements and split up again with some rapidity causing 'ethnic' confusion to Classical historians – and probably to themselves. Thus, for some Classical writers, 'Celts' and 'Gauls' may have been used as specific terms implying distinct ethnic identities. For the most part the terms were probably more loosely employed, much as today we might use the words Greek and Roman or, for that matter, American.

Until the beginning of the fourth century BC direct knowledge of the Celts of temperate Europe was limited, but from then on the Mediterranean world had ample opportunity to observe them first hand. To begin with they were encountered as migrants, raiders, and mercenaries, some moving through the Alpine passes to settle in the Po valley and attack Italy beyond, others trekking from the Middle Danube into the Balkans, Greece, and Asia Minor. Later the Romans confronted the Celts as native peoples in their own lands to be conquered and governed, as the Imperial armies spread into Iberia, across Gaul, and into the Upper and Middle Danube valleys. These various encounters, for the most part aggressive, allowed the Mediterranean world to observe Celts, often in very large numbers, at close quarters. It also required them to create a philosophical framework in which to present and understand these frightening people from the north.

As barbarians, Celts were, of course, 'other' – different from 'us' and therefore to be characterized in a way that could be easily understood. Their barbarous – that is their non-Mediterranean – attributes and behaviour had to be stressed. What emerged was a caricature – and like all caricatures the Celtic stereotype was generalized, selective, and exaggerated – yet it contained a basis in reality.

Plato, in his *Laws* written in the middle of the fourth century, is the first to offer observations on the Celts stressing their warlike nature and their drunkenness. He may have been making his own observations first hand among the mercenaries employed by Dionysius of Syracuse in conflicts on the Greek mainland. Mercenaries, however, are not always the best ambassadors for their culture and therefore Plato's comments may be biased, but these two aspects of Celtic behaviour became a recurring theme. Strabo, for example, is quite explicit:

> The whole race . . . is war-mad, high spirited and quick to battle, but otherwise straightforward and not of evil character. And so when they are stirred up they assemble in their bands for battle quite openly and without forethought . . . They are ready to face danger even if they have nothing on their side but their own strength and courage. (*Geog.* 4.4.2)

Strabo was probably using the lost ethnographic works of Poseidonius as a source for this and much of his other information on Celtic behaviour, and, since Poseidonius is thought to have travelled in the West, probably in Gaul, in the late second century BC, he too may have made first-hand observations rather than just repeating earlier sources.

Poseidonius is probably the source for the account published by Diodorus Siculus of Celtic wine-drinking. Of the Celts in Gaul he writes: 'They are exceedingly fond of wine and sate themselves with unmixed wine imported by merchants; their desire makes them drink it greedily and when they become drunk they fall into a stupor or into a maniacal disposition.' That Roman wine was indeed imported in great quantity to the Gauls at that time is shown by the huge quantity of wine amphorae found on Gaulish sites. Diodorus is no doubt reporting, if second hand, an actual observation, but, by stressing that they drank their wine unmixed, he was pointing up how different the barbarian Celts were to the civilized Mediterraneans, who preferred to dilute their wine. The Celts may drink our wine but they are 'other'.

Bravery in war and drunkenness are the two things that every Roman student would have learnt about the Celts. But Celtic bravery had to be distinguished from Roman bravery. Thus, says Strabo, they may be open and high spirited but they are also childishly boastful and they wear lots of gold and flashy clothes. 'It is this vanity which makes them unbearable in victory and so completely downcast in defeat.' However true these statements may have been, he presents them deliberately to point up the contrast between Celt and Roman. The Celts are valiant but they are boastful exuberants and easily become totally demoralized. The Romans are also valiant but they are sober, self-controlled, and steadfast.

The Classical texts abound with anecdotes displaying the Celt as 'other'. Aristotle, for example, mentions homosexuality as being openly approved of among the Celts, tells us that they toughen up their children by immersing new-born babes in cold rivers and by giving them little clothing, and notes, rather obscurely, that the Celts take up arms against the sea. Ephorus (quoted by Strabo) offers the insight that the Celts are careful to avoid becoming fat or pot-bellied and a young man is punished if his stomach hangs over his belt. Another sketch that would no doubt have got a laugh from

Poseidonius (*c.*135–*c.*50 BC)

Poseidonius was a Syrian Greek polymath born in Apamea on the river Orontes. He studied in Athens and eventually settled in Rhodes, where he established a school dedicated to Stoic philosophy, which became famous throughout the Mediterranean world. Pompey and Cicero were among the many who studied there. His writing covered a wide range of subjects besides philosophy – astronomy, mathematics, geography, zoology, botany, anthropology, and history were among the topics he was known to have tackled. Some time about 90 BC he set out on a journey to visit the central and west Mediterranean. His itinerary naturally included Italy and Rome, but he also travelled extensively in Spain and southern Gaul and it is here that he came into contact with Celts. One of the purposes of his extensive travels was to collect material for his great work *Histories*, which was to chart the development of the Roman world from 146 BC probably to the mid-80s. It was a major study in fifty-two books but survives now only as quotations in the works of later writers. It was Poseidonius' ethnography of the Celts that provided the information for Strabo, Diodorus Siculus, Athenaeus, and possibly also Caesar. As a Stoic philosopher Poseidonius chose to present the Celts as 'noble savages' – he has been called a soft primitivist.

a Roman schoolboy is Diodorus' description of the long drooping moustaches of the Celts, so long that they completely cover the mouth so that drink is strained through them. Assuming these vignettes to be accurately observed, it is impossible to say how widespread such behaviour patterns were.

While most of the Classical writers describing Celts would have subscribed, perhaps unconsciously, to the Celt-as-other stereotype, each writer would have introduced additional biases depending on the agenda he was writing to. For Aristotle, Plato, and Ephorus it was simply a matter of showing that barbarians were different from Greeks, but, after the Greek and Roman world had come into direct conflict with Celts during the migrations and their aftermath in the fourth and third centuries, the stereotype was refined. The leitmotif now was that the wild fearless warriors from the north tested the mettle of the Mediterraneans and honed their greatness. To writers like Polybius, Livy, and Pausanias it provided the opportunity of showing the triumph of their worlds and their values – civilization over savagery, order over chaos. The otherness of the Celts had to be emphasized, and perhaps distorted, while at the same time their prowess as a noble and worthy foe had to be built to such a point that Greek or Roman victory could be presented as a great triumph. Once established, the metaphor of the danger coming from the north was ever present in the Roman mind.

Others, too, used their victories over Celts as a symbol of their own greatness. Pergamum – a powerful Hellenistic city state in western Asia Minor – did so with particular skill. After an attack on Delphi in 279 BC, a large group of Celts had moved into Asia Minor and eventually settled in the centre of the region where Ankara is now located. From here raiding parties terrorized the surrounding territories, particularly the Greek cities of the Aegean coast: only Pergamum was strong enough to resist. After initial successes in the 220s, the king, Attalus I, set up a large victory monument in the sanctuary of Athena in Pergamum depicting Gauls in defeat. It was from this group that the famous sculpture of the dying Gaul, known from what is usually thought to be a later Roman copy, originally came. Another showed a Gaul, supporting the body of his dead wife, committing suicide. Here was a noble foe indeed.

Later, after the final defeat of the Gauls, between 168 and 166 BC, the Pergamene rulers made more exaggerated claims. In the temple

1. The Dying Gaul: a Hellenistic vision of a Celt. The statue, now in the Capitoline Museum, Rome, is thought to be a Roman copy of an original that adorned a victory monument erected in Pergamum in the late third century BC.

of Zeus at Pergamum a great altar was set up adorned with a triumphant sculptured frieze. A vigorous scene presenting the gods Zeus and Athena defeating the Giants was counterbalanced with an equally monumental depiction of the Attalid rulers overcoming the Gauls. The symbolism was clear for all to see. To take the message to an even larger audience a victory monument was erected on the acropolis of Athens. This time the reliefs showed the Pergamene defeat of the Gauls balanced with the Greek defeat of the Persians at Marathon and mirrored by mythological scenes of Greeks against Amazons and, by implication, the ancestors of the Pergamenes against Titans. The Attalid claim to be the saviours of Hellenism against the forces of chaos and thus the natural heirs of the Greeks would have been hard to miss. It is doubtful, though, that a Celtic chieftain leading a summer raiding party to the Aegean coast would have recognized himself in the guise of such an exalted enemy of civilization.

The defeat of the Anatolian Gauls in the 160s saw the end of the Celts as a serious threat to the Graeco-Roman world. Twenty years or so earlier the Celts living in the Po valley had been subdued by Rome and new Latin colonies were established there. Protected by the Alps, Rome could at last breathe a sigh of relief and the metaphor of the Celts could begin to be rewritten.

Foremost among the revisionists was Poseidonius, a Stoic philosopher from the Syrian town of Apamaea who lived c.135–c.50 BC. His great work, now lost apart from quotations by others, was a history taking the story of Rome on from the point in the mid-second century where Polybius' history had ended. One of the events he dealt with was the Roman conquest and annexation of Gallia Transalpina (roughly modern Provence and Languedoc) in the last decades of the second century. Here Rome had come into direct contact with Celtic tribes, and in one of his books Poseidonius produced an ethnographic account of the natives based, in part at least, on his own travels.

Poseidonius, so the later commentator Athenaeus tells us, structured his account 'in accordance with his philosophic conviction'. In other words the Celts were now viewed through the distorting lens of Stoic beliefs presenting them as rather beguiling 'noble savages'. They were brave and honoured valour in others, they showed unquestioning hospitality to strangers, and they were ruled by just priests (the Druids). True they drank a lot, were prone to be rowdy at times, and had a few curious habits like collecting human heads, but they 'were not of evil character'. Such peoples, in the eyes of Poseidonius, were, in their simplicity, far closer to the Golden Age than was his own civilized society. Thus the image of the Celts was beginning to change; no longer were they the vicious enemy from without but were neighbours prepared to enter into political allegiances and, perhaps more to the point, people you could do business with. Diodorus Siculus (probably quoting Poseidonius) sums it up succinctly: 'many Italian merchants with their usual lust for profit look on the Gallic love of wine as their treasure trove. They take the wine by boat on the navigable rivers and by wagon through the plains and get in return for it an incredibly large price: for one amphora of wine they receive a slave – a servant in exchange for a drink.'

In the middle of the first century BC (59–51 BC), when Julius Caesar was pursuing his Gallic Wars in an attempt to extend the frontier of the Empire northwards to the Rhine, the Celts he encountered, as allies and as enemies, are presented surprisingly dispassionately. One is given the impression of a high degree of organization and of social and political sophistication, at least among the tribes closest to the Roman territory of Transalpina. The different tribes pursued their own political agendas but would come together for mutual support and defence when times required and charismatic figures emerged to lead them. Caesar's presentation of his enemies was subtly contrived to reflect his own glory, but his depiction of the Celts of Gaul in the first century probably comes reasonably close to the reality. Through his eyes we are seeing barbarian society in a state of rapid change. The Celts were well on the way to becoming friends embraced by Rome. Beyond lay a new enemy – the Germans: it was they who now fulfilled the role of the uncivilized barbarians without.

Chapter 3

A little prehistory: the Atlantic *longue durée*

We have seen that the Classical writers, in so far as they gave any precision at all, regarded the Celts as among the westernmost peoples of Europe. Herodotus is quite explicit about this, implying that only the Cynetes, on the western coast of Portugal, lay between them and the ocean. The Celts of Gaul were also an ocean-facing people. On this Julius Caesar is quite clear, telling us, in the famous opening paragraph of his *De bello gallico*, that 'the Celts are separated from Aquitani by the river Garonne, and from the Belgae by the Marne and Seine'. The language spoken across this swathe of Gaul had close similarities to that spoken throughout much of central and western Iberia at the time and is ancestral to the 'Celtic' languages spoken in Brittany, Cornwall, Wales, Scotland, and Ireland in recent times. It is for all these reasons that we need to look, as dispassionately as possible, at the cultural development of western Europe throughout the *longue durée* of the prehistoric period.

A glance at the map of Europe, suitably adjusted to jolt our cognitive geography, is sufficient to stress that Atlantic Europe is a cohesive region. Its many promontories and peninsulas are linked by the ocean, while the flooded valleys of its ria coastlines provide sheltered waters reaching deep inland. The great rivers of France and Iberia flowing westwards into the ocean are arteries of

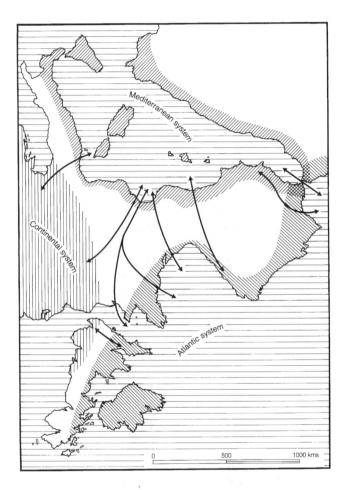

2. The Atlantic seaways. The map emphasizes the importance of the
Atlantic façade of Europe as a zone linked by sea travel.

communication binding huge swathes of inland territory to the littoral zone.

That there is a significant degree of coincidence between Atlantic Europe defined in these strictly geographical terms, and the extent of the Celts glimpsed through the Classical texts and the distribution of the Celtic language groups, is clearly a matter worthy of further exploration.

The importance of the Atlantic seaways as a means of communication first becomes apparent in the sixth and fifth millennia BC in what is traditionally called the Mesolithic period. At this time, for the coastal communities, the sea was an important resource. Not only was the coast exploited but so too was the deeper water, to judge by the size of fish hooks used and the type of fish caught, implying that seagoing vessels were now in use, though we know little of them. The Mesolithic networks of exploitation may not have been extensive, but if shoals of fish were being followed on a seasonal basis then regular patterns of movement involving periodic landfalls will have brought disparate communities into contact, allowing technologies to be shared and beliefs and patterns of behaviour to spread along the ocean façade.

By the fourth millennium, after animal husbandry and crop cultivation had been introduced into the region, evidence of the exchange networks linking communities becomes more readily apparent. One of the more dramatic demonstrations of this is provided by the distribution of polished stone axes made of diorite from Plussulien in central Brittany. The axes were manufactured and distributed on a massive scale, no doubt using routes by sea and along the major rivers, in particular the Loire and the Seine. Nothing is known of the social context of this exchange but in all probability the axes embodied high prestige, far above their pure utility, and changed hands in the cycles of gift exchange, which enabled communities to articulate socially.

Belief systems linking concepts of the cosmos and attitudes towards death and ancestors also spread widely along the Atlantic façade, as the distribution of megalithic monuments and tombs has long shown. In recent years precise radiocarbon dating and a more sophisticated analysis of these monuments have shown them to reflect an Atlantic phenomenon owing nothing to Mediterranean inspiration. In the fourth millennium the main centres of innovation were scattered along the Atlantic, in the Tagus region of Portugal, the Morbihan in southern Brittany, the Boyne valley of Ireland, and the Orkney Isles. Although each region had its own distinct characteristics, the degree by which they shared concepts of architecture, art, cosmology, and belief is remarkable. While we no longer have to believe in 'megalithic missionaries' proselytizing along the Atlantic shores, what this stunning display of shared culture implies is the rapid and continuous spread of ideas through the long-established social networks that bound the ocean-facing communities and the filtering inland of these practices along the river routes. The third millennium saw the continuation of this pattern with the appearance, dissemination, and assimilation of a particular set of cultural attributes usually referred to as the 'Beaker package'. This 'set' included the concept of single burial of the deceased accompanied with a beaker-shaped pot and a selection of other artefacts, which might include arrows, wrist guards, copper alloy daggers, and personal ornaments such as gold earrings. For a long time it was believed that the spread of this package across much of central and western Europe was the result of the migration of 'Beaker folk', but most archaeologists now believe that what we are seeing are the local manifestations of a belief system which became rapidly disseminated through the exchange networks that had developed over the preceding three millennia.

Among the earliest of the beakers are those called Maritime Bell Beakers, which are found in some considerable concentrations in the Tagus region and the Morbihan – a distribution echoing the innovative centres that had emerged more than a millennium earlier. It is quite possible that the type first developed in one, or both, of these regions, linked as they always had been by coastal exchange networks.

The third and second millennia saw the increasing exploitation of raw materials, particularly gold, copper, tin, amber, and ornamental stone such as jadeite. Such commodities were valued because of their rarity and were, in all probability, distributed in systems of elite exchange. The rareness of these commodities and their uneven occurrence gave particular prominence to certain locations and routes.

The Atlantic zone was especially well provided. The heavily mineralized pyrite zone of western Iberia offered copper and silver in the south and gold and tin in the north. Brittany and south-west Britain were sources of tin and yielded gold and copper as well, while a zone stretching across southern Ireland to north Wales was an important source of copper, with gold coming from the Wicklow mountains. Once copper alloys came to be widely used for tools and weapons in the third millennium the demand for copper and tin intensified dramatically. With this came increased exploitation and an intensification in exchange.

The working of these systems along the Atlantic is amply demonstrated by the distribution of different kinds of artefacts spread along the coastal routes. Copper alloy tanged points, known as Palmela points, made in the Tagus region reach as far north as southern Brittany. Lunulae (neck ornaments) of Irish gold reach Cornwall, Normandy, and Brittany, while the gold Berzocana neck rings of south-west Iberia are found in Brittany and northern Britain and Northern Ireland. These few examples, chosen from the many more that could have been quoted, demonstrate the vitality of the Atlantic networks.

From the thirteenth century until the seventh century BC (that is the Late Bronze Age and beginning of the Iron Age) the extraction and distribution of metals intensified still further – a fact amply demonstrated by the very large quantities of tools and weapons in circulation, many of which ended up buried in hoards or thrown into lakes, rivers, or bogs in fulfilment of some ritual imperative. So much material survives in the archaeological record that it is possible to chart, and often to quantify, the region of origin and the distribution gradients of individual types. Thus the distinctive sword type known as the Carp's Tongue sword occurs in great quantity in Brittany, where it was clearly manufactured, and from there swords were distributed along the Loire and the Seine and across the Channel into south-eastern Britain. Slightly different versions of the same basic type were made in the Charente and at least two different sites in southern Spain. This must mean that Breton examples were transported southwards and were sufficiently prestigious to encourage local smiths to copy them, introducing minor modifications of their own. What we are perhaps seeing here is not just the exchange of artefacts but the transmission of concepts of value.

The sword would have been one of the pieces of equipment by which the elite warrior displayed his status. There are, in the south-west of Iberia, stone stelae of the eighth or seventh century, which may originally have commemorated dead warriors. Many of them are carved to depict the deceased along with the equipment proclaiming his status – a four-wheeled vehicle, a sword, spear, and shield, and other items more difficult to identify but possibly brooches and mirrors. The swords sometimes resemble the profiles of Carp's Tongue swords, while the shields were depicted as circular with concentric raised ribs and studs as would befit a shield with a beaten bronze face. The concentric raised ribs are shown with a V-shaped interruption characteristic of the so-called V-notched shields.

The south-west Iberian stelae are unique, but the V-notched shields they depict are known from several sites in western Europe, and a very fine example in leather was recovered from a bog in

Co. Longford in Ireland. The Atlantic distribution of the shields reflects the distribution of certain sword types (like the Carp's Tongue swords) and also distinctive varieties of spears. What all this suggests is that the warrior elites of the entire Atlantic region shared the same value system, even, in some cases, to the design of the weapons themselves.

One element of this aristocratic society seems to have been its penchant for feasting, the feast providing an important occasion for establishing and reaffirming the social hierarchy and for negotiating agreements and alliances. The feast would have focused around the hearth, furnished with spits for roasting meat, cauldrons for stewing it, and flesh hooks for lifting the hot joints. Bronze examples of all three are known in western Europe with a predominantly Atlantic bias, coming from Britain and Ireland and from the western part of France and Iberia. These feasting sets, comprising highly specialized equipment, reflect a very distinctive behaviour pattern, which the distribution so dramatically shows to be Atlantic.

The sets of warrior equipment and the feasting gear combine to give an integrity to the Atlantic zone stretching from south-western Iberia to Scotland, suggesting that, over the entire region, not only were the exchange networks working intensively but also that behaviour and beliefs were being widely shared.

The introduction of iron as the everyday metal of tools and weapons does not appear to have disrupted, in any significant way, the traditional culture of the Atlantic zone except that the burial of bronzes in hoards placed in the ground came to an end. Since the majority of bronzes known in the Atlantic zone come from hoards, the superficial impression that this gives is that the bronze industry came to a spectacular halt. But several things are mixed up here and need to be teased out. The first is that bronze certainly continued to be used on a large scale and the demand for copper and tin continued unabated, but whereas, until around the seventh century, much of the Atlantic bronze was consumed locally or found its way, through recycling, into the markets of west central and northern Europe, from this time onward the Mediterranean seems to have become a demanding new market that preferred to have its metal delivered in ingot form. Thus, there is no reason to suppose that the volume of production or distribution diminished.

The end of 'hoarding' is, however, interesting. It is often argued that the majority of the hoards were votive deposits and that the reason that the belief developed was really economic – to remove metal from circulation in a time of increasing overproduction. This may have been so, in which case the development of new markets in the Mediterranean ready to absorb the surplus may have been the stimulus to allow the old beliefs, demanding hoarding, to wither away.

Whatever the truth behind these complex issues may prove to be, the fact remains that the core of the traditional belief system continued intact. The chthonic deities residing in watery places continued to be revered and offerings of weapons and other gear continued to be deposited into the bogs, rivers, and springs even into the first centuries AD.

Sufficient will have been said in this rapid sketch to show that the sea played a crucial role in the distribution of materials and in linking communities together across very considerable distances, but this does not necessarily imply that very long journeys were made by sea. A better way to characterize how the systems probably worked is to visualize the Atlantic coast as a continuous corridor from Morocco to the Shetland Isles along which large numbers of people were travelling but always on short-haul journeys. In such a system, while the people might have ventured only tens of kilometres, ideas and beliefs could pass quickly from one end to the other. Much the same picture holds true for the major river routes. By these corridors the Atlantic coastal communities were in direct communication with the hinterland of Iberia and west central

Europe and, through these zones, with the Mediterranean world beyond.

Large-scale folk movements have played no part in this story so far. Forty years ago they would have, but the old invasionist/ migrationist paradigms so popular in the nineteenth and early twentieth centuries seldom feature in modern archaeological reasoning. This is not to say that movements of population did not take place – clearly they must have done – but simply to stress that recent research has tended to focus on continuity and the persistence of indigenous populations, and to explain culture change as coming about through the dissemination of ideas across the networks of exchange, invigorated by localized innovation.

When the communities of Atlantic Europe are considered together through time, it becomes apparent that, far from being a distant, benighted periphery to the bright and beautiful Mediterranean, it was throughout a cohesive cultural zone with periods of spectacular development built on home-grown innovation.

So how can we bring this archaeologically constructed picture into juxtaposition with the question of the Celts?

The languages spoken in these regions, at least from the sixth century BC, belong to the group that scholars have, from the beginning of the eighteenth century, chosen to call 'Celtic'. Could it be that, far from being a language introduced by invaders or migrants moving in from central Europe, it was the language of the indigenous Atlantic communities, which had developed over the long period of interaction beginning in the fifth millennium BC? It may not be irrelevant in this context to remember that many of the peoples considered to be Celts by the early Classical writers lived in the Atlantic zone of mainland Europe, in Iberia and in France, in territories where their ancestors may have lived for hundreds of generations. Let us leave the implications of this hovering until more evidence has been assembled and explored.

Chapter 4

A little more prehistory: the elites of middle Europe

To complete our survey of the prehistoric background of those areas of Europe that may have some claim to being the homeland of the Celts we must consider what archaeology has to show of west central Europe – a zone roughly coincident with eastern France and southern Germany. From a geographical point of view this region, stretching northwards from the north flank of the Alps, is exceptionally well endowed. It is here that the great rivers of Europe (Danube, Rhine, Rhône, Saône, Seine, and Loire) come close together, creating a gigantic route node. Assuming that the river valleys provided the easiest means of communication, the west central European zone occupied the point where the main east–west route, ultimately joining the Black Sea and the Atlantic, was crossed by north–south routes from the west Mediterranean and Adriatic to the English Channel, North Sea, and Baltic. Communities occupying such a location had the opportunity to become powerful and innovative.

In the Late Bronze Age (*c*.1300–800 BC) west central Europe began to develop a sufficiently characteristic culture to allow it to be distinguished from other regions within the broad continuum usually referred to as the Urnfield culture. In this North Alpine Zone hillforts begin to proliferate and among the very large numbers of urned cremations found in many cemeteries a few can be distinguished, by virtue of their included grave goods, as belonging to an elite. One of the classes of artefacts that hint at status are the bits and side pieces of horse harness representing either riding horses or the pairs of beasts used to pull the four-wheeled vehicles that may have accompanied funerary processions.

The use of the horse and of the four-wheeled vehicle in burial rites has a very long ancestry in the east of Europe and in the Pontic steppe and beyond, and it is tempting to see the appearance of these attributes in the North Alpine Zone as the result of developing communication providing the elites of the region with an exotic model of behaviour that they could adopt to distinguish themselves from those of lesser status.

In the eighth and seventh centuries (called the Hallstatt C period in archaeological nomenclature, and firmly now iron-using), the elite come more sharply into focus in the archaeological record because of their adoption of the inhumation rite, which means that their grave goods were buried with them rather than being destroyed on the funerary pyre. Now these richer graves are usually identified by four-wheeled vehicles, probably funerary wagons, buried with the deceased in a large pit together with other items of equipment including sets of horse harness, and usually a long slashing sword. These Hallstatt C wagon burials extend in a comparatively narrow zone from Bohemia across southern Germany and reflect the nucleus of a rather broader region within which warriors of lesser status were buried with their distinctive iron swords but without the elite symbol of the wagon. If the concentration of iron swords is taken as the indicator of this core cultural group, then the zone covers the entire region from Bohemia to Burgundy and from the Alps to the Middle Rhine.

It is difficult to model the social complexity of so large a region from the archaeological evidence alone, but that society was hierarchical is implied by the different grave sets that can be readily identified. After six or seven centuries of stability it is likely that the population had remained largely static, inheriting ancestral territories in lines of unbroken succession going back for generations, while the relationships between the individual communities would have been maintained in a degree of harmony by long-established networks of obligation. It is quite possible that by this stage the many discrete polities that constituted the Hallstatt C core zone regarded themselves as a single people.

The sixth century saw a further stage in their development that makes the Hallstatt elites even more archaeologically recognizable. This came about as the result of developing links with the Mediterranean, which allowed distinctive manufactured goods from the Greek and Etruscan worlds to be drawn northwards into the courts of the chieftains. The contacts developed slowly. The pioneers were the Etruscans who, in the seventh century, had established trading entrepôts on the southern coast of France around the Golfe de Lion at sites like Saint-Blaise at the mouth of the Rhône. While the economic imperative of this would have been to trade with the coastal communities and the immediate hinterland, occasional trade goods found their way further north. Towards the end of the seventh century Greeks from the coast of Asia Minor began to explore these waters and about 600 BC established a trading post of their own at Massalia (Marseilles). By the middle of the sixth century the Greek enterprise was beginning to dominate the region, and imported goods such as bronze wine-drinking equipment and Attic pottery cups (both Black Figured and Red Figured ware), together with locally produced Massaliot wine carried in distinctive amphorae, begin to appear more widely in the archaeological record, not only in the coastal zone and the Lower Rhône valley but now more frequently on the Hallstatt sites of west central Europe.

By what mechanisms these luxury items were drawn northwards it is very difficult to be sure. It is quite conceivable that the more elaborate, like the great bronze krater from Vix, were diplomatic gifts taken to the courts of the northern chieftains to establish good relations in order to facilitate trade – one scholar has half-jokingly referred to them as 'introductory offers'. From the point of view of the native elites, ease of access to luxury goods provided a new way to display their exalted status in life as in death, and it is no surprise, therefore, that the Mediterranean imports are found both in the defended hilltop settlements such as Mont Lassois and Heuneberg and in the burials of the paramounts like the individuals interred with wagons and other elaborate gear at Vix, Hochdorf, and Homichele. These rich Hallstatt D burials and the contemporary hilltop settlements ('seats of nobility', as they are sometimes called) form a compact zone stretching from Burgundy to Baden Württemberg – some 600 kilometres east–west and 200 kilometres north–south – which encompasses the headwaters of all the major rivers. The wealth of the society is vividly demonstrated not only by the distribution of Mediterranean imports but by the extensive use and deposition of gold.

The social system that enabled these elites to maintain themselves has been called a 'prestige goods economy'. The argument goes that the elites enforced their right to be the only individuals able to receive luxury goods from outside the system. Some of these exotics, as well as valuable goods generated within the system, were then handed down the various levels of the hierarchy as gifts from patrons to clients in return for services.

In such a system the paramount chieftain would probably have acquired the exotic Mediterranean goods through middlemen acting as ambassadors for the Mediterranean partners, the feast being the occasion when the gifts were bestowed and gifts of equivalent value offered in return. These are most likely to have been raw materials such as gold, amber, tin, salt, furs, as well as manpower in the form of slaves. All these commodities could have been acquired within the zone or in the peripheral regions to the north and west.

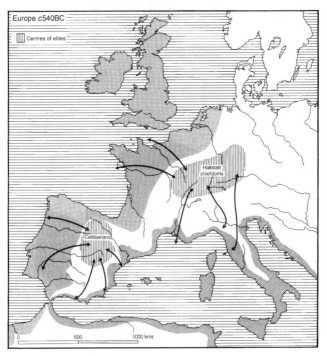

3. Systems at work in Europe about 540 BC.

The socio-economic system, as it is sketched out here, seems to have been comparatively short lived, developing around about 540 and coming to an end around 480 BC. In other words the equilibrium, such as it was, was maintained for only two or three generations. Why the system came to an end and the west Hallstatt elites faded from archaeological visibility is difficult to say with any degree of certainty, but in all probability it was due to a number of factors triggered by a reorientation of the exchange systems with the Mediterranean world.

One factor of direct relevance was the expansion of the Etruscan sphere of influence extending from Etruria northwards through the

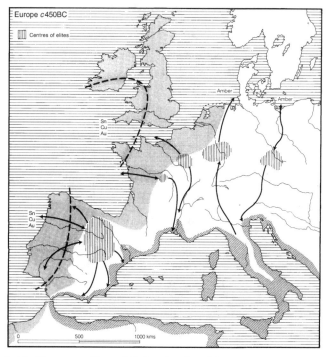

Europe c450BC

Centres of elites

Amber
Amber

Sn
Cu
Au

Sn
Cu
Au

0   500   1000 kms

4. The European elites and their networks c.450 BC.

Apennines into the Po valley in the period between 520 and 480 BC, allowing the development of regular trade through the Alpine passes to the barbarian north. This is signalled by the rapid development of Como, one of the settlements on the main trading route through the mountains, and the appearance in elite graves to the north of comparatively large quantities of Etruscan bronze vessels, in particular beaked flagons and stamnoi. These were probably made in Etruscan towns like Vulci in the period c.480– 420 BC. What is particularly noticeable about their distribution in west central Europe is that they tend to turn up in the graves of a newly emerging elite occupying a broad zone around the northern periphery of the old Hallstatt D chiefdoms. In the archaeological nomenclature these burials belong to the La Tène A or La Tène I period. The change of name does not imply that there was any great dislocation or movement of population: it simply reflects the cultural changes and social readjustments taking place in the early fifth century BC.

Various possible scenarios could be offered to explain the emergence of the La Tène elite. One would be to see it triggered by the northward expansion of Etruscan trade at this time. The very dense distribution of Etruscan beaked flagons in the Middle Rhineland, between the Rhine and Moselle, looks as though a deliberate link was established between Etruria and this region. Such a development may have upset the delicate balance that underpinned the earlier prestige goods economy upon which the Hallstatt D chiefdoms depended. Another possibility, which does not exclude the first, is that the communities commanding the major route nodes and resources around the periphery of the main concentration of Hallstatt D chiefdoms became more and more powerful. Four distinct groupings of early La Tène elite burials can be recognized. The largest is in the Moselle region, with another of lesser extent 200 kilometres to the west in the area of the Marne: smaller concentrations occur in Bohemia and in the vicinity of Bourges. Each dominates one of the major river routes to the west and north.

One simple way to explain both the Hallstatt and early La Tène elites is in terms of the economic interaction of the consuming Mediterranean and the resource-rich barbarian west and north. As Mediterranean demand increased in the seventh century BC, the long-established Hallstatt elites were able to control the through flow of commodities and manpower, but after two or three generations it was the communities who commanded specific resources that were able to benefit. The Bourges group had access to Atlantic tin, while the Bohemian chieftains commanded the major amber route from the Baltic. For the Moselle and Marne it may have been a variety of resources, gold, iron, salt, and slaves, that enabled them to flourish. Thus the new centres of power emerged around the periphery of the old in the same way that mushroom rings grow outwards from the original pioneer colony.

The new early La Tène chiefdoms, while retaining some of the characteristics of their Hallstatt D predecessors, differed in a number of ways from them. Those La Tène burials, accompanied by a vehicle, now favoured a two-wheeled chariot-like construction that may have been inspired by Etruscan vehicles. Another significant difference was the prevalence of weapons in the La Tène graves. Many of the male deceased, not only the elite, were accompanied by their swords and spears and occasionally helmets. In the Hallstatt D chieftain burials the normal 'weapon' was a dagger that was more appropriate to hunting and feasting than to fighting. While the trappings of the feast were still present in the form of Etruscan flagons and stamnoi and Attic cups, and sometimes roasting spits, the emphasis of the early La Tène burials was on the military prowess of the dead warrior. Evidently the social basis of the emerging elites was very different from that of their predecessors.

Why this should have been is a matter of speculation, but one possibility is that the communities occupying the territories around the old Hallstatt core area were involved in raiding to acquire slaves and other commodities that they exchanged with the paramounts of the core. The increasing demand for goods would have exacerbated these warlike tendencies, thus offering the mechanism by which the successful war leader could rise to dominance.

The courts of the elites in the Marne and Moselle regions also provided the patronage necessary for the spectacular development of craft skills and in particular a highly distinctive art style usually referred to simply as Early Celtic Art. From the outset it was an aristocratic art designed to adorn the possessions of the rich. Among the earliest pieces it is possible to see the different elements

5. The grave of one of the early La Tène elite found at Somme-Bionne in the Marne region of northern France in 1873.

from which the craftsmen gained their inspiration. The forms of the vessels owed their origin to Etruscan prototypes, while formal Etruscan motifs like the palmette and arabesque are rapidly transformed into the vigorous scrolls, tendrils, and leaf motifs that are made to flow with such ease at the hands of the native metalworker. Some inspiration was also gathered from the animal art of the east, perhaps from the Scythian communities of the Great Hungarian Plain or beyond. To begin with, the animals and their stylistic ancestry are quite evident, as with the beasts decorating the gold arm ring from Rodenbach, but later they merge into the curvilinear exuberance of the transformed foliage. Whereas the earliest Celtic Art is still formal with heavy reliance on bilateral symmetry, it soon erupts into an exuberant asymmetry. In the unemotive terms used by art historians, the *Early Strict Style* gives way to the *Free Style*.

Celtic Art has sometimes been treated by archaeologists as though it were a separate subject to be studied in isolation, divorced from all social contexts, whereas, in reality, art styles are deeply embedded in society, reflecting its beliefs and values. Thus the adoption of an art style is more than just the random borrowing of decorative motifs – it is rather the embracing of a culture in all its complexity. Leaving aside isolated items dispersed through exchange networks, it could fairly be argued that communities adopting the values reflected in the art style we choose to call 'Celtic', by integrating them into their own material culture, are proclaiming their acceptance of a set of common cultural values. Whether or not this can be taken as a claim to a common ethnic identity raises questions to which we shall return.

Chapter 5
Peoples on the move

The movement of Celts from north of the Alps into the Mediterranean lands in the period from about 400 BC is amply documented by Greek and Roman historians writing several centuries after the events. The sources are sufficiently detailed to provide an outline history of the various migrations and raids and to offer some insight into the nature of the communities involved and the fighting methods of the warriors. That said, it must be remembered that our two principal sources, Polybius (*c*.204–122 BC) and Livy (59 BC–AD 17), were writing to specific pro-Roman agendas and readily adopted, and indeed embellished, the established Celtic stereotype. Nevertheless, they will have had access to sources no longer available and the basic history of what they have to offer can be broadly accepted.

Livy gives a simple sketch of how the migrations began. They originated in Gaul under the leadership of the Bituriges and were sparked off by overpopulation. The king, Ambigatus, chose his two nephews to lead the exodus, and, after consulting the augurs, one led his people eastwards through the Black Forest and Bohemia, while the other moved south into Italy. 'Taking with him the surplus populations – Bituriges, Arverni, Senones, Aedui, Ambarri, Carnutes, Aulerci – he set out with a vast host, some mounted, some on foot' (*Hist.* 5.34). Once through the Alps they established a settlement at Mediolanum (now Milan). A later writer, Pompeius

Trogus, adds that some of the 300,000 Gauls involved in the migration moved on, past the head of the Adriatic, to settle in Pannonia (modern Hungary).

Livy dates the coming of the Gauls to about 600 BC, while Polybius places it 200 years later. This apparent contradiction can be explained by supposing that the initial movements may have begun, as Livy suggests, about 600 with the infiltration of small groups through the Alpine passes and their settlement in the southern foothills of the Alps in the vicinity of Lake Como and Lake Maggiore. This was the territory of the (archaeologically named) Golasecca culture, which can be shown to have been exchanging goods with the Hallstatt communities to the north. A southwards drift of population is not unlikely and indeed there is some archaeological evidence to support the idea of Celtic settlement in the fifth century on the southern fringe of the Golaseccan sphere. It is even possible that Celts were deliberately settled there to provide a buffer against the expansionist interests of the Etruscans. This bow wave of Celts seems to have turned into a surge at the end of the fifth century.

Polybius provides an account of the main migrations, naming the individual tribes and explaining how they gradually colonized the Po valley, those arriving later passing through the already-claimed territories to settle beyond, until the latest to arrive, the Senones, moved far south to fill up the last remaining land between the Apennines and the Adriatic. The archaeological evidence adds some support to this account, enabling individual tribal groups to be identified, and in some cases to be related, through their burial rituals, to their homeland territories north of the Alps. According to Polybius, the Celtic settlers lived in villages and were engaged in 'war and agriculture'. Wealth was measured in cattle and gold, while a man's status was reflected in the size of the entourage he could persuade to serve under his patronage.

The bald outline of the story sketched by the Classical writers is no doubt a great oversimplification of a complex reality, but it is generally consistent with the rather softly focused archaeological evidence.

The sources are unanimous in their belief that overpopulation was the prime cause of migration and that people were drawn south into the Po valley by their knowledge of all the good things that were to be had there – specifically mentioned are dried figs, grapes, oil, and wine. This second point is easily understood in terms of the long-established exchange networks, which saw the export of Etruscan wine-drinking gear, among other commodities, to the north from the late sixth century onwards. These archaeologically visible items must reflect only a small fraction of the southern luxury products reaching the north.

The question of population pressure is more difficult to approach, but there is ample evidence in the Marne and Moselle regions to suggest that the fifth century saw a consistent and quite dramatic rise in population. In these areas, as we have seen, the elite constituted a warrior aristocracy and the implication is that warfare, in the form of raiding, was embedded in the social system. In a situation in which there was a steady increase in population, it is easy to see how raiding expeditions may have become increasingly ambitious, with the young war leaders having to take their followers further and further from the homeland. A system of this kind has a built-in trajectory of escalation. It would only be a matter of time before some leaders moved from the homeland for good and established themselves and their followers in distant territories. Once begun, the momentum would have increased, drawing populations away to colonize new ecological niches from which to raid new territories. Some such dynamics could have provided the motor for the Celtic migrations, beginning with small-scale movements in the sixth century and reaching a crescendo of colonization by the end of the fifth century. That both the Marne and Moselle homelands give the appearance of having undergone some degree of depopulation in the fifth century adds further support to the scenario.

Once settled in the Po valley, the Celtic communities seem to have continued with their raiding lifestyle. Polybius stresses their attachment to warfare and mobility and indeed there is ample historical evidence of Celtic raids to the south. The Etruscan town of Clusium was attacked in 391 BC, and a year later Celtic bands had ravaged much of the growing city of Rome and were holding the remaining parts, including the Capitol, under siege. Thereafter raids continued on and off for much of the next 150 years. During this time there were roving bands as far south as Apulia.

While the general pattern, at least at first, may have been of organized raids taking place each year during the summer season, with the warriors returning home to the Po valley with their booty in the autumn, contact with the Mediterranean states created new opportunities, which led to modifications in the Celtic systems of aggression. As early as 385 BC we hear of Celtic warriors, no doubt under the command of their own war leaders, being enlisted at Ancona in the territory of the Senones, by Dionysius of Syracuse to serve as mercenaries in his campaigns. Over the next thirty years he and his son used Celtic mercenaries both in Italy and in Greece.

The presence of a large Celtic population in the Po valley provided a reservoir of fighting men, and during the Second Punic War (214–202 BC) Hannibal relied, somewhat unsuccessfully, on Celtic mercenaries in his campaigns in Italy. After hostilities had ceased, Rome realized that the Celtic threat had to be dealt with once and for all. The Cenomani were forced to conclude peace in 197 BC and, after a number of campaigns and the founding of colonies, by 183 BC the Po valley – Cisalpine Gaul – was effectively under Roman control.

Livy's account of the beginnings of the Celtic migrations described an eastern movement, apparently along the Danube valley. There is

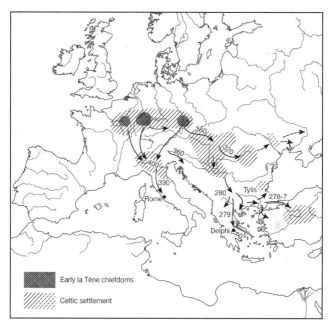

6. Movements of the Celts 400–270 BC attested by historical sources and by archaeology.

no further historical record of them, but by 335 BC Celtic communities had reached the Balkans (though it is possible that they may have arrived via the Po valley). We know of this because a group of Celtic emissaries from the Adriatic region paid court to Alexander the Great to negotiate a treaty of friendship and hospitality.

The archaeological evidence suggests that Celtic groups, presumably using the Upper Danube valley, moved, in some number, into the Middle Danube region during the fourth century, settling on both sides of the river in Transdanubia and the Great Hungarian Plain (both now Hungary) and extending downriver to around the confluence of the Drava and Sava in modern Serbia. Other groups moved further east into Transylvania in the heart of what is now Romania. All of this is attested by the appearance of artefacts of La Tène type and the adoption of La Tène burial practices, but of the nature of the movements we are largely ignorant.

In the Bohemian homeland there is some archaeological evidence to suggest complex population movements, with some land being abandoned, perhaps as the result of outward migration, and new groups from the west moving in to take over. In this period of upheaval and mobility, migrants, raiders, and displaced populations may have merged together in a single eastwards flow, re-forming themselves into new configurations as land was taken and settled. The part played by the local populations in all this is obscure, but there can be little doubt that the communities that emerged from the mêlée of the fourth century would most likely have incorporated a high percentage of the indigenous peoples. Thus, although the appearance of the material culture is predominantly La Tène, the genetic mix may have been very different. The population of the Middle Danube is usually referred to as Celtic by Classical writers and by archaeologists: it is as well, however, to bear in mind that 'celticized' is probably a more appropriate word to describe the new tribal configurations that emerged.

The meeting between the Celtic emissaries and Alexander in 335 BC (at which the Celts are reported to have made their famous statement that they feared only that the sky might fall on them) is a reminder that the Macedonian state controlled a substantial part of the Balkans and as such formed a barrier to further Celtic expansion. With the death of Alexander in 323 and the political instability that ensued, new opportunities for raiding and expansion presented themselves. In 298 Celtic raiders, led by Brennus, thrust into Thrace and Macedonia but were vigorously repulsed. Later, in another raid in 280, a force of Celts and Thracians succeeded in killing a Macedonian commander and paraded his head on a spear. The victory paved the way for a more audacious raid in the following year, when a very substantial force

Brennus (d. *c.*278 BC)

Brennus (though the name may be apocryphal) was the leader of a massive raiding force of Celts – said to number 40,000 – that rampaged through the Balkans in the unsettled period following the death of Alexander the Great. In 279 BC his force overran Macedonia and moved south into Greece, attracted by a knowledge of the wealth protected in the precinct of Apollo at the sacred site of Delphi. At Thermopylae the invaders were checked by the Greeks. Brennus divided his force into three, sending one detachment to pillage Aetolia, thus drawing the Aetolians away from Thermopylae and allowing the Celts to break through. While the Celtic detachment in Aetolia and another led by Acichorius were harassed by Greeks using guerrilla tactics, Brennus reached Delphi and besieged the sanctuary. What then happened is unclear – the Greek sources are reticent – but in the end snowstorms and falling rocks demoralized the Celts and during an engagement Brennus was wounded. Eventually the force retreated northward but was harassed by the Thessalians, at which point Brennus, the failed leader, committed suicide. It was the remnants of his force that, with others, crossed into Asia Minor. Their descendants were still recognized as a distinctive people in the first century AD when St Paul, in an epistle, addressed them as 'Oh foolish Galatians'.

pushed southwards into Greece to the sanctuary of Apollo at Delphi. They were attracted, says Pausanias, by the 'wealth of the Greek States and the even greater wealth in the sanctuaries including votive offerings and coined silver and gold'. What ensued is unclear, but Delphi appears to have been largely unscathed and the Celtic force, disheartened by earthquakes accompanied by thunder and lightning, gave up their siege and retreated northwards.

While it is certainly true that the death of Alexander and the consequent weakening of Macedonian power provided the opportunity to raid Greece, it may not have been the direct cause. After all, the Celtic tribes of the Middle Danube appear to have been quiescent for several generations before the onslaught. However, in the twenty years or so before the raid, the Romans had been advancing against the Senones living along the Adriatic coast and in two battles, in 295 and 283 BC, had decisively defeated them. The move will have caused much upset, not only among the Senones but also among the other Celtic tribes in the Po valley, who would have appreciated that their turn was soon to come. Many will have decided to move away and it is quite conceivable that the wave of new migrants swept eastwards through Slovenia into the Middle Danube. If so, this could have been the catalyst for the new phase of raiding culminating in the massive attack on Greece in 279.

The failure of the raid saw the immediate fragmentation of short-lived Celtic confederacy. Some stayed in Greece to serve as mercenaries, some moved back into the Middle Danube region, and another group settled in Thracian territory close to the Black Sea. Many, however, stayed on the move, crossing the Hellespont and the Dardanelles to seek their fortunes in Asia Minor.

The Celtic presence in Asia Minor made itself felt for more than three centuries, from the first arrivals in 278 BC until the middle of the first century AD, when St Paul penned his Epistle to the Galatians – the name by which the Celtic communities were generally known. Even as late as the fourth century AD something of their distant ancestry may still have been discernible in their language, which St Jerome said reminded him of the language of the Treveri living around Trier – though it is possible that Jerome's memory was conditioned by his prior knowledge of the Celtic ancestry of the Galatians.

The Celts who poured into Anatolia in the third century BC were not simply warrior bands looking for action. One account records that, out of a force of 40,000, half comprised women, children, and old men no longer fit for service. This evidently was a folk movement requiring land to settle, while their combatant menfolk could seek employment as mercenaries in the service of the local Hellenistic rulers or engage in their traditional raiding activities. The first homeland was a barren highland area by the river Halys in northern Turkey, from where they raided at will. Later, after being resettled in the centre of Anatolia (in a territory around modern Ankara), their raiding resumed, focusing now on the rich cities of the Aegean coastal region, until they were soundly defeated in about 233 BC by the Pergamene king Attalus I. In the years to follow Celtic warriors found service with the Seleucid and Ptolemaic rulers and played a significant part in the battle of Magnesia in 190, when they and the Seleucid king, Antiochus III, were defeated by the Roman and Pergamene army. As part of the terms imposed by the victor, the Galatian tribe agreed to cease raiding, but in 167 they began once more to attack Pergamene interests and it was only decisive action by the Pergamene ruler Eumenes II that finally brought them to heel (and provided Eumenes with the excuse to build his great victory monuments at Pergamum and at Athens).

Although we have a rich body of reference material – textual and sculptural – to attest the Celtic presence in Asia Minor, there is surprisingly little material culture that is recognizably La Tène in character. This must mean that, when the personal items they brought with them had been used up, they were content to adopt local products. They were, after all, moving into a region technically and culturally more advanced than the area from which they had come. In battle, however, it would seem that they retained their traditional weapons and practices: the monument erected in Pergamum after the Celtic defeat of 233 BC depicts weapons that are distinctly La Tène in character, and even as late as 190 some of the Galatian fighters were going naked into battle, as, forty years or so earlier, some of the Celts fighting in Italy chose to face the enemy. While at first sight this might seem to suggest a conservatism spanning three or four generations, it remains a possibility that, throughout this period, bands of Celts from the Middle Danube valley continued to make the crossing to Anatolia to join kinsmen already there. Whether or not this was the case, some sense of ancestral identity seems to have been maintained.

The folk movements we have discussed spanning the period 400–200 BC are those for which there is some direct textual evidence. Inevitably these focus on interactions with the Graeco-Roman world. Given the degree of mobility characteristic of the time, it would be surprising if there were not other movements around the northern and western fringes of the initial early La Tène core zone. There are hints of this in similar tribal names. The Parisi(i) are found in the Seine valley and eastern Yorkshire, while the Tectosages was the name of a tribe that crossed into Asia Minor after 279 and one that settled around modern Toulouse. In both cases there is cultural evidence which could be thought to reflect some direct relationship. At best it is a reminder that the situation was complex and our evidence is often partial in the extreme.

Chapter 6
Talking to each other

The archaeological evidence we have explored above shows quite decisively that across much of western Europe stable communities existed over long periods of time, often bound together by networks of exchange. The testimony of the Classical writers, with some support from archaeology, adds a different dimension by sketching the complex movements of peoples from west central Europe southwards and eastwards, as they fought their way into Mediterranean history after about 400 BC. During the *longue durée* of indigenous development and the frantic chaos of folk movement, people needed to talk to each other: the language they used, in its various forms and dialects, belongs to a group that, since the beginning of the eighteenth century, philologists have called 'Celtic'.

It might be assumed that after 200 years of scholarship the origins and development of the early Celtic languages would have been pretty well understood, yet in his essay 'The Early Celts: The Evidence of Language', a recent and enthusiastic review of Celtic philology by one of its greatest practitioners, David Ellis Evans concludes 'that this scholarly activity has, by and large, not produced the results that are generally acceptable and enlightening. The labyrinthine and frustrating nature of the subject discussed here must not be denied or disguised, for all the new insights gained from caring concentration on it.' With that warning in mind let us proceed cautiously.

Celtic language studies really began in Oxford at the end of the seventeenth century with the researches of Edward Lhuyd (see also p. 116). Lhuyd worked at the Ashmolean Museum, first as Assistant Keeper and, from 1691 until his death in 1709, as its Keeper. Of his many contributions to scholarship, his greatest was in the field of comparative linguistics. By 1695 his research had reached such a point that he felt able to prepare a prospectus for the great work of synthesis he intended to publish, *Archaeologia Britannica*. In it, he said, he wished to compare the Welsh language with other European languages, Greek and Latin, naturally, but also the neighbouring languages of Irish, Cornish, and Armorican. *Archaeologia* was to be a multi-volume work, but in the event only the first volume ever appeared, in 1707. Its aim, he wrote, was to present a 'clearer notion of the first planters of the three kingdoms and a better understanding of our ancient names of persons and places'. To enable his readers to understand the original sources, written in Irish and 'British', it was necessary to provide some linguistic tools. Thus Volume 1, entitled *Glossography*, presented grammars and vocabularies of Irish, Breton, and Cornish. These languages, together with Welsh and Gaulish, he chose to refer to as 'Celtic'.

Lhuyd noted, and discussed in his correspondence, the close similarities between Welsh, Cornish, and Breton and their difference from Irish (this was later to be systematized as the difference between P-Celtic and Q-Celtic), and to explain this he began to develop a historical model that, after 1700, he was debating with his friends and was prepared to sketch in the preface of the Welsh edition of *Archaeologia*. He envisioned an initial colony of invaders from Gaul moving into Britain, but later being forced out, to Scotland and Ireland, as a second wave of invaders from Gaul moved in. In Ireland they mixed with the indigenous Scotti, who had earlier arrived from Spain and some of whom later crossed into what was to become Scotland.

Here, then, we have the origins of the invasionist model that lies at the basis of the belief, still held in some circles, that Celtic invaders from the Continent introduced the Celtic languages into Britain and Ireland. It is predicated on the arguments that the languages of Britain and Ireland were introduced from the Continent and that they were the same as the languages spoken by people described by Classical writers as Celts. Both arguments, it must be stressed, are *assumptions*.

In 1882, Sir John Rhŷs, Professor of Celtic at Oxford University, published an influential book, *Early Britain: Celtic Britain*. Building on Lhuyd's pioneering work and the scholarly discussions that had followed, he formalized the invasion theory by concluding that a migration of Q-Celtic-speaking Goidelic Celts from Gaul settled in the British Isles, some spreading across to Ireland. Later, P-Celtic-speaking Brythonic Celts arrived in southern Britain, ousting the earlier settlers, who fled into western areas of Britain and into Ireland. After he had clearly stated the theory, it was then left to archaeologists to provide the supporting cultural evidence and to offer dates.

So much for past theories: now let us examine what the linguistic evidence has to tell us in the light of more recent research. The Celtic languages belong to the Indo-European family of languages and are, for convenience, divided into two groups: Continental and Insular. Continental Celtic, as the name implies, was spoken on the mainland of Europe and, apart from Breton, which presents some complications (considered below), is now no longer extant. It is known largely through personal and place names recorded on coins, in the works of ancient historians and on inscriptions, and from a few (very few) longer inscriptions, which give the briefest hints of the structure of the language. From this all-too-sparse record it is possible to distinguish three distinct groups: Gaulish, Celtiberian, and Lepontic. A scattering of Celtic place names and personal names is also found throughout the Middle Danube valley and in Asia Minor. These names probably result from the migratory movements beginning in the fourth century BC, but they are attested only in later contexts and tell little of the language spoken in these areas.

The Insular Celtic languages were, and in some places still are, spoken in Great Britain, Ireland, and Brittany. As we have seen above, it has been conventional to divide them into two groups, Q-Celtic or Goidelic and P-Celtic or Brythonic. The distinction is made on the basis of the pronunciation (and thus the spelling) of the *qu* sound. In Q-Celtic it remains as the hard *q-* or later *k-*, whereas in P-Celtic it softens to *p-*; thus in Irish 'four' is *cethir* and in Welsh *pedwar*. Although much was made of this distinction in the past, modern philologists have tended to play it down, stressing that it is only one, and perhaps not the most significant, of the differences between the various constituents of Insular Celtic. That said, Q-Celtic is spoken in Ireland, the Isle of Man, and western Scotland, while P-Celtic is spoken in Brittany and Wales and was, until *c.*1800, also spoken in Cornwall. It also seems to have been the language of the rest of Britain before its gradual replacement by Germanic and Romance languages after the middle of the first millennium AD.

The great value of Insular Celtic is that it is still a living group of languages that can be studied as such and the histories of which can be traced back through a succession of earlier texts. Something of the complexity of these studies is, however, well demonstrated by two examples: Gaelic and Breton.

Scottish Gaelic and Manx, both Q-Celtic languages, are generally believed to have been introduced by folk movements from Ireland in the third or fourth century AD, for which there is good historical evidence. It is, however, possible that both regions spoke Q-Celtic already and the historical invasions simply reinforced the indigenous language.

Brittany presents a rather more complex problem. Historical tradition has it that between the fifth and seventh centuries AD

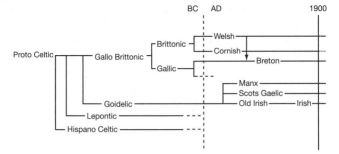

7. A diagram to illustrate how the Celtic language group is thought to have developed.

communities migrated from south-west Britain to settle in the Armorican peninsula. For a long time the conventional view was that these communities reintroduced P-Celtic into an area where Latin had, over the four centuries or so of the Roman occupation, replaced the original Celtic language. More recently, however, these views have been challenged. In the 1950s François Falc'hun suggested that the British migrants encountered an Armorican population who still spoke Gaulish, which was closely akin to Brittonic. Thus, instead of reintroducing Celtic to Armorica, the incomers simply strengthened the language that had survived the period of Romanization. Falc'hun further argued that the dialect of Breton spoken by the Vannetais in the south-east of the peninsula differed from that of the rest of the country because it was a purer form of Gaulish unmodified by the British dialect, the implication being that British immigrants did not settle in that area. Léon Fleuriot, writing in the 1980s, argued that for much of Brittany the dialects spoken were the result of a Brittonization of the indigenous Gaulish but preferred to see Vannetais as Gaulish influenced by Latin.

These two examples are a salutary reminder of the linguistic complexities that can arise when even small groups of people are on the move and of the difficulties experienced in trying to untangle them even when dealing with a living language.

For the rest of Europe, outside the Armorican peninsula, whatever residual spoken Celtic may have survived during the Roman period, it is reasonably certain that the last remnants would have been erased in the course of the subsequent Migration Period between the fifth and eighth centuries. All that now remains are the few inscriptions and the names given by Classical writers or embedded in recorded place names: it is a meagre harvest.

Of the Continental Celtic languages, Gaulish is the best known. Apart from the place names and personal names recorded by Classical writers, most notably Julius Caesar and Strabo, there are a significant number of Gaulish inscriptions written in Greek or Latin script. For the most part they are graffiti scribbled on pots or on dedicatory inscriptions. But great excitement was occasioned in 1971 when a lead tablet was found in the sacred spring in Chamalières. Written in Roman cursive, it was at the time the longest Gaulish text, comprising 336 characters mostly making up personal names. In 1983 a longer text of 1,000 characters (160 words) was discovered at Larzac near Aveyron. It too was inscribed on lead and appears to have been a magical text, including some reference to female magicians, but the text remains in part obscure. Taken together, the evidence for the Gaulish language is not particularly extensive, but it is sufficient to suggest that, by the second and first centuries BC, Gaulish was spoken over most of what is now France.

In Iberia the situation is more complex. As we have seen, early Greek writers believed that some, at least, of the inhabitants of western Iberia were Celts. By the third century BC, according to Eratosthenes, they had become more numerous, and by the second and first centuries BC *Celtiberi* are frequently referred to. Diodorus explains the name as the result of the fusion of two tribes after a long and bloody war, but this has the ring of guesswork about it.

It is clear from a variety of evidence, but mostly place names and a few inscriptions, that a Celtic language was spoken over much of central and western Iberia. This is particularly well demonstrated by place names ending in *-briga*, which are found over much of the peninsula except for the eastern zone and Andalucía, where the non-Indo-European languages of Iberian and Tartessan were prevalent. Within the 'Celtic' area, different language groups have been identified, of which Celtiberian and Lusitanian are the two best defined. There is much debate about the significance of these different groups. Some scholars would argue that Lusitanian, which extends along the Atlantic coast of the peninsula, is not a Celtic language at all, but others would see it as an archaic form of Celtic. With such a limited database to work on, it is doubtful if questions of this kind will ever be satisfactorily resolved.

The third area where direct evidence of the Celtic language has been recorded is in northern Italy, where, it is argued, the few inscriptions that are at present known can be divided into two distinct groups. The earliest group, found in the region of Lugano, around the Italian lakes, have been named Lepontic and of these the earliest have been dated to the sixth century BC. The later group are in Gaulish, though written in Lepontic script, and are presumably the work of the Celtic groups who penetrated the area from about 400 BC onwards. The early group are particularly interesting, since they could be thought to add support to Livy's date of *c.*600 BC for the first Celtic infiltration from the north. As we have seen, the archaeological evidence for the area (the Golasecca culture) suggests that in the sixth and fifth centuries the communities on either side of the Alps had established close contacts with each other.

Given the fragmentary and disparate nature of the evidence for the Celtic languages, it is hardly surprising that attempts to create a grand historical synthesis, even at the schematic level of a simple family tree, have seldom met with much success. There are, however, several simple generalizations that most would agree are valid. The first is that Gaulish and Brittonic (that is, the P-Celtic

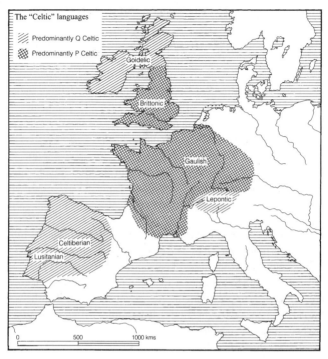

The Celts

8. **Regions of Europe where Celtic languages developed.**

group) are very similar and may have developed at the same time with both regions being in contact. Goidelic (the Q-Celtic of Ireland, the Isle of Man, and western Scotland) shares many characteristics with them but is more archaic. The second point is that Lepontic and Celtiberian, in comparison with Gaulish and Brittonic, are also archaic in structure and form. Slightly more contentious is the suggestion that, if one arranges these languages in relation to their similarity to the 'more developed' Gallo-Brittonic, then the sequence would be Celtiberian–Lepontic–Goidelic, with Celtiberian being the most 'archaic'.

There are, of course, many ways in which this set of relationships, assuming them to be valid, could be explained, but the simplest would be to accept, as a basic premiss, that the Celtic languages developed in western Europe in the region where later they are to be identified – that is, central and western Iberia, Gaul, Britain, and Ireland – the broad similarity between them resulting from the long-established contacts between these regions along the Atlantic seaways and the Atlantic-flowing rivers that provided routes to the interior. As we have seen, there is ample archaeological evidence to show that these regions were bound in a network of exchange systems probably starting as early as the fifth millennium BC and reaching a peak of high intensity in the Late Bronze Age, c.1300–800 BC.

After 4,000 years of interaction, involving not just a movement of goods but a flow of knowledge and beliefs, it is not unreasonable to suppose that there will have been a convergence in language, and it was, perhaps, in the period of intense contact in the Late Bronze Age that the Celtic language took on the earliest form we know (and sometimes characterize as Q-Celtic). That it was spoken throughout the region, no doubt in many different dialects, is shown by the fact that this early form has been identified in Iberia, Ireland, and the Lepontic region as early as the sixth century.

This is a convenient place to pause. We will return again to the question of language later, in Chapter 11, when we try to bring together some of the different threads of evidence.

Chapter 7
Telling stories

In most societies throughout time, listening to the tales of storytellers played a crucial part in everyday life. The stories provided a sense of the inherited past, they informed about the dangers and temptations of life, and they provided a set of moral standards that the listener was invited to accept. No less important was the occasion itself – the coming-together of family and friends sitting around the hearth engaged in the common pursuit of reflecting on their shared heritage.

Storytellers were still practising their art in remote parts of Ireland in the twentieth century. The folklorist J. H. Delargy gives a moving description of his encounters of one such, Seán Ó Conaill, a 70-year-old farmer-fisherman who lived in a two-roomed cottage in the hamlet of Cíllrialaig in Co. Kerry in the 1920s. Although technically illiterate

> he was one of the best-read men in the unwritten literature of the people whom I have ever known, his mind a storehouse of traditions of all kinds, pithy anecdotes, and intricate hero-tales, proverbs and rhymes and riddles, and other features of the rich orally preserved lore common to all Ireland three hundred years ago. He was a conscious literary artist. He took a deep pleasure in telling his tales; his language was clear and vigorous, and had in it the stuff of literature.

There can be little doubt that the storyteller practised an ancient art and that many of his stories, passed on from generation to generation, reflected the actions and mores of a long-distant past. There would have been an imperative to retain the accuracy of the narrative by memorizing it word for word. Julius Caesar, writing of the Druids, notes that 'during their training they learn by heart a great many verses, so many that some people spend twenty years studying the doctrine'. He was clearly impressed by such feats of memory, unfamiliar in a literate society.

The need for accuracy in memory is emphasized in a colophon added to the text of the Irish saga *Táin Bó Cuailnge* (*The Cattle Raid of Cooley*), recorded in the twelfth century in the *Book of Leinster*. It promises 'a blessing on everyone who will memorize the *Táin* with fidelity in this form and will not put any other form on it'. There is then a presumption that the stories told should retain their integrity and form, but for all this there will have been additions and updatings, explanations in parentheses, and literary flourishes added for effect. The tale told at any one moment will have been a many-layered construct rather like an archaeological site with its strata accreted over time. The best-known examples of this are the Homeric sagas, the *Odyssey* and the *Iliad*. Written down in the eighth century BC, they reflect the final state of a complex oral tradition built up over five centuries or more of retelling.

In 1964 Kenneth Jackson, Professor of Celtic at Edinburgh University, gave the Rede Lecture at Cambridge. His title was 'The Oldest Irish Tradition: A Window on the Iron Age'. It was published in the same year and has since then provoked a lively debate. Jackson's thesis was that the Irish saga *Táin Bó Cuailnge* contained within its basic structure much that reflected heroic society in pre-Christian Ireland about AD 400 and that this allowed the workings of earlier Celtic society to be glimpsed. Subsequent scholarship has cast some doubts on the details of the argument. Jim Mallory, for example, has shown that much of the material culture described in the *Táin* is that of the sixth to ninth centuries AD and has nothing at all to do with the Iron Age. Others have gone so far as to deny that the stories, preserved in the medieval manuscripts, are in any way close to the earlier oral form, if indeed it ever existed. Yet, if we accept all the reservations, there still remain within the *Táin* some remarkable correspondences with the society of Celtic Gaul as recorded by Poseidonius (135–50 BC).

The Irish vernacular literature, recorded in medieval manuscripts, divides into four groups, the Mythological Cycle, the Ulster Cycle, the Fenian Cycle, and the Historical Cycle. It is the Ulster Cycle that concerns us here. It is a collection of about eighty stories, of which the longest is the *Táin*. The others comprise either scene-setters that provide a background for the main saga or separate stories enlarging on the activities of some of the main characters. The entire corpus is contained in ten manuscripts varying in dates, partial but overlapping.

The earliest version of the main story (Recension I) has been constructed from two manuscripts, *The Book of the Dun Cow* written in the eleventh century and *The Yellow Book of Lecan* dating to some three centuries later. Recension I is thought to have been derived from texts of the ninth century, no longer extant, which may themselves have been based on texts of two centuries earlier. There is another more complete version of the story (Recension II) in the *Book of Leinster* dating to the late twelfth century.

The saga, then, after an unknown period of telling and retelling, was finally written down, perhaps as early as the seventh century, by Christian scribes and transcribed on a number of occasions in scriptoria across Ireland. No doubt, during this process, changes will have been made, like the modernizing of the material culture, and elements offensive to Christian susceptibilities excised or at least watered down. It may have been at this stage that allusion to, and imagery from, the Homeric sagas were introduced by erudite monks. What emerged after 500 years or so of literal transmission is likely to have been significantly different from the oral saga first transcribed and yet much would have been faithfully transmitted. The monastic scribe who wrote out the text of the *Táin* in the *Book of Leinster* adds a telling footnote of his own:

> But I who have written this history, or rather story, do not give faith to many of the things in this history or story. For some things therein are delusions of the demons, some things are poetic figments, some are like the truth and some are not, and some are for the amusement of fools.

The story of the *Táin* begins with 'pillow talk'. King Ailill and Queen Medb are in bed in the fort of Cruachan and talk turns to the wealth that each has contributed to the marriage. They compare like for like, each matching the other until Ailill mentions his great bull, Finnbennach the White Horned. Medb cannot equal him and 'her spirits fell as though she were penniless'. Not to be outfaced, she makes enquiries and, hearing that there is a match – the Brown Bull of Cooley – in the province of Ulster, she sets out to acquire the beast. And so the great cattle raid begins.

The story that follows tells of the conflict between the raiding party from Connacht and from other parts of Ireland led by Medb against the men of Ulster ruled by King Conchobhar from the royal centre of Emain Macha. Both sides field the best of their warrior aristocracy. Among Conchobhar's force we are introduced to experienced warriors like Ferghus mac Roich and Conall Cernach, headstrong young men like the principal character Cú Chulainn, the wise Sencha mac Ailella, and Bricriu the poison-tongued who creates tensions and rivalries to suit his own interests. The Druid Cathbhadh also plays a significant role.

As the saga nears its end, Cú Chulainn kills Ferdia in single combat. Ferdia turns out to be his foster brother, giving the engagement a particular poignancy, but not long after Cú Chulainn dies of his wounds. In the final scene the contest is repeated. The Brown Bull of Cooley brought to Connacht in triumph kills Finnbennach the

Cú Chulainn (uncertain)

Cú Chulainn is a character who recurs in the tales of the Ulster Cycle. The tales are mostly concerned with the Ulaidh, who ruled Ulster, the northern part of Ireland, which at the time extended from Donegal in the west as far as Antrim, Down, and Louth in the east. The capital was at Emain Macha, from where King Conchobhar ruled. Cú Chulainn, son of Sualtam, was one of the heroes of the men of Ulster. He is depicted as a semi-divine personage under the special protection of the god Lug, who in some texts is said to be his father. Cú Chulainn is the epitome of the hero – good-looking, brave, and selfless, with a heightened sense of honour. He has humour and forbearance but can be dreadful when roused. He fights from chariots, cuts off the heads of enemies, and is passionate about single combat – all the characteristics of a Celtic hero in the Poseidonian tradition. His most famous role, in the *Táin Bó Cuailnge*, is as the defender of Ulster at the time of the great conflict with the Connachtmen led by the formidable queen Medb. At this time the Ulstermen are under a spell that has sapped all their energy: only Cú Chulainn and his father are free from the curse and it is Cú Chulainn who almost single-handedly beats back the enemy advance. In the surviving vernacular literature the character has been rewritten and aggrandized. Whether or not a real historical figure lurks here or just an 'eponymous hero', it is impossible to say. As one might expect, Cú Chulainn has taken on a cult significance among some Ulster factions today.

White Horned but dies worn out by the ferocity of the contest. Thereafter Ulster and Connacht settle down in peace and 'for seven years after none of their people was killed in Ireland'.

In a work as complex and finely woven as this there are many different levels at which it can be read. Is it, as some have suggested, a reflection of a long-forgotten bull cult, or is it an allegory to enliven the listeners' understanding of the deities conceived to be opposites in balance – male:female, earth:sky, and so on – and the chaos that can be unleashed when the balance is knocked out of equilibrium? The only answer is possibly.

At a different level there is the closely written and highly detailed social context within which the action is played out. It is a warrior aristocracy of young lords bound by rigorous rules of behaviour. Honour and prowess in battle are paramount. Personal prestige is jealously guarded and offence quickly taken. The feast is a bonding institution where hospitality is displayed and status reasserted in the ritual of the hero's portion when cuts of meat symbolizing an individual's place in the hierarchy are publicly offered and sometimes contested. In warfare the individual lord is the central figure often engaging in single combat. Chariots feature large and the severed heads of enemies are taken as trophies. Social relationships are equally carefully drawn. Women can be powerful and serve as war leaders; the dowries of husbands and wives are held in common and the fosterage of children among the elites was the norm, providing an assured way of maintaining some degree of harmony in a society where tempers could be short.

The social system embedded within the Ulster Cycle tales bears remarkable similarities with that of Gaulish society described by Poseidonius at the beginning of the first century BC and to a lesser extent by Caesar fifty years later. The correspondences are so close that it is difficult not to accept that both sprang from the same tradition.

Perhaps the most striking is the hero's portion. The Poseidonius tradition records it thus:

> And in former times when the hindquarters were served up the bravest hero took the thigh piece and if another man claimed it they stood up and fought in single combat to the death. Others in the presence of the assembly received silver or gold or a certain number of jars of wine and having taken pledges of the gift and distributed it among their friends and kin, lay stretched out face upward on their shield, and another standing by cut their throat with his sword.

In this rather abbreviated account, Poseidonius seems to conflate two stories that had been told to him about the way the Celts of Gaul used to behave – The Hero's Portion and The Champion's Bargain. The Hero's Portion is a theme central to two of the stories of the Ulster Cycle, the *Story of Mac Dathó's Pig* and *The Feast of Bricriu*. In the former the main action takes place at a feast where the Connacht champion Cet mac Mágach, after pouring scorn and abuse on the Ulstermen present to bolster his own prowess, has won the right to carve the pig. At this moment the Ulster hero Conall Cernach enters. The two men contest the right to carve and eventually Cet concedes that Conall is the better warrior, but adding, 'If it were Ánluan who were in the house, he would contest with you. It is bad for us that he is not in the house.' 'But he is', Conall replied and, taking a severed head from his belt, hurled it at Cet. Conall then turned his attention to carving the pig. Taking the best joint for himself, he gave the forelegs to the Connachtmen, thus insulting them. In the ensuing mêlée the floor became heaped with corpses and the next morning the blood was still flowing over the threshold.

The Feast of Bricriu is also built around the manipulation of The Hero's Portion, but the second theme, The Champion's Bargain, is also introduced when Cú Chulainn and his rivals are invited to cut off the Giant's head but have to allow their own heads to be cut off. As the story develops, Cú Chulainn stretches himself out waiting for the moment, just as the Gaul lay on his shield in the story that Poseidonius recounts in a somewhat incredulous way.

Poseidonius had been told the story by a source who may simply have been passing on a folk tale he had heard rather than reporting an act he had witnessed. In any event, the similarities between the Gaulish and Irish traditions strongly suggest a common source, whether it be oral tradition or observed behaviour.

Chariots feature large in the *Táin*. From the text it is clear that the kind of vehicle described was two-wheeled and consisted of a light wooden frame. The wheels were probably spoked and had iron tires. The vehicle was pulled by two yoked horses and was driven by a skilled charioteer who carried the warrior to his place of battle. This kind of chariot was seen by Julius Caesar when campaigning in Britain. He was greatly impressed by the skill of the charioteer and the manœuvrability of the vehicle, which allowed the British force to combine the 'mobility of cavalry with the staying power of infantry'. Poseidonius records similar chariots in Gaul two generations earlier, and in both Britain and Gaul there is ample archaeological evidence in the form of chariot fittings and horse gear, and in some places actual chariot burials, to provide firm support for the Classical texts. But surprisingly not so in Ireland, where the archaeological evidence for chariots is almost entirely lacking. While it is as well to remember the old archaeological adage that absence of evidence is not evidence of absence, the possibility must be allowed that the use of the war chariot was never a feature of Irish Iron Age society.

So where does this leave us? The sagas and stories of the Ulster Cycle are a source of incomparable value, the core of which must originate in an Iron Age milieu – this much is clear. But is it an Irish milieu? Could it be that Irish names and places have simply been grafted on to an ancient pan-European folk tale reflecting a heroic age, some time between the fifth and second centuries, acted out somewhere in the La Tène cultural zone of west central Europe? A story of such power, embodying heroic ideals, could not fail to capture the imagination and would have spread quickly and widely, to be taken up by even the most far-flung of the communities who embraced aspects of the La Tène belief system. Whatever the explanation, it is little short of a miracle that the tradition, overlaid with Irishness, has survived.

Chapter 8
Sharing values

All communities live within a culture – a set of shared values expressing their identity. Cultures are complex, but essentially they reflect the beliefs and values of the social group and usually embody some sense of the past and aspirations for a future. An anthropologist or sociologist can approach culture through direct communication with the group under study. A historian has more limited access through the filter of the written word, while an archaeologist dealing with the more distant past has to rely largely on surviving material remains, sometimes with the addition of distorted anecdotes that come down to us through scraps of contemporary writing. Fifty years ago the definition of a prehistoric culture seemed comparatively straightforward: works of that period are rich with culture names – Michelsberg culture, Beaker culture, Urnfield culture – but now archaeologists are more circumspect, realizing that definitions such as these, while generally useful as broad archaeological constructs, may have little reality when attempting to understand how past communities defined their own identity.

Is there such a thing as 'Celtic culture'? The answer must be no. If, for the sake of this argument, we take the three communities who are thought to have spoken an early form of Celtic language in the sixth century BC – those living in the centre of the Iberian peninsula, in the Lepontic region, and in Ireland – there is little in the material culture of these three regions to suggest a commonality of values sufficient to imply any significant degree of cultural unity. Indeed, it is quite likely that these disparate people would not even have been able to understand each other's speech. Their sense of identity would have been based on their lineage groups and upon larger social constructs, which for convenience we can call tribes, and some of the tribes might have come together in allegiances and confederations to which names might have been given, but in no sense would they have thought of themselves as part of a 'Celtic nation'.

In the fifth century, as we have seen, things began to change. The emergence of La Tène 'culture' with its focus in the Marne–Moselle region, and the subsequent migrations to the south and the east, spread a 'package' of ideas far and wide across Europe. The continuing mobility of peoples in the fourth to second centuries and activity through existing trade networks encouraged and intensified the exchange of ideas. As a result, elements of the La Tène 'culture' can be found across much of middle Europe from Ireland to the Black Sea. It is understandable, therefore, that some writers have accepted the assumption that La Tène culture, archaeologically defined, and Celts, as portrayed by Classical writers, are synonymous. It is for this reason that the art style prevalent in La Tène contexts is generally referred to as Celtic Art. This shorthand nomenclature, used for the convenience of making simple generalizing statements, can lead to unsupported assumptions. We must try to unpack some of these preconceptions.

That there is a reasonably coherent package of beliefs and values that can be called La Tène culture is a useful generalization. It encompasses a set of burial traditions, both inhumation and cremation, in which the deceased is interred in a single grave, usually with a range of personal equipment, the graves being arranged in cemeteries. Those assumed to be males are often accompanied by weapons, including swords, spears and shields, while those thought to be women may have armlets and safety-pin brooches. There are, it should be stressed, many exceptions to these generalizations and a wide range of regional variations, but quite close similarities do exist over surprisingly large areas. Burials as far afield as the Marne, the Po valley, and Transylvania recognizably belong to the same general tradition and imply similar values and beliefs held by these disparate communities.

The decorative styles used (that is, the Celtic Art) tell much the same story. The archaeological evidence shows how the repertoire of the La Tène craftsmen developed in the service of the elites of the Marne and Moselle regions in the fifth century and thereafter spread rapidly. In the fourth century continuing contact between the communities settled in the Po valley, and those remaining in the Transalpine homeland ensured that new ideas inspired by Etruscan culture filtered through to be incorporated in the fast-evolving and increasingly distinctive schools of La Tène craft activity.

Celtic Art was far more than purely decorative art-for-art's sake. The choice of motifs and their arrangement will have held meaning for those who could interpret them. It is highly probable that they communicated identity and status as well as endowing the owner with a degree of divine protection. The symbolism of the boar, for example, is widely in evidence – on helmet crests found from Romania to the suburbs of London, on shields from the river Witham and from southern France, and stamped on a sword blade from Switzerland. It is tempting to see the boar as a talisman used to ward off danger or to give added strength to the bearer.

The human head is also frequently depicted enmeshed in the swirl of other motifs. Superb examples are the pair of terret rings from a horse harness, found in northern France and now in the Musée National des Antiquités in Paris. Once the eye knows what to look for, the heads jump out from their background of flowery scrolls. The great art historian Paul Jacobsthal jokingly referred to this as

9. Human faces incorporated into the design of two rein rings of La Tène date, found in northern France.

the 'Cheshire Cat Style' – sometimes in the tree you can see the whole cat and sometimes just the grin of the cat! Stare hard at the shield facing dredged from the river Witham and you will suddenly see doe-eyed horse heads with wings instead of ears, or contemplate the circular shield boss from the Thames at Wandsworth and the swirling tendrils will resolve themselves into two fearsome birds. It is very much an art of dreams, where things are not quite as they should be and where shapes transform themselves without warning. Shape shifting of this kind is a recurring feature in the Insular vernacular literature.

There is another aspect worth considering. Distinctive motifs give the object bearing them an identity and with identity it can accumulate a history. Thus it is quite likely that a distinctive helmet or shield or a sword in its decorated scabbard would have been known and talked about – even revered. A weapon used in famous conflicts to kill exalted enemies could not fail to accumulate an aura of power. So great might it become that it was fit only for the gods and would end its life sacrificed to them. Some such system may explain why so many items of prestige armour have been found in rivers and bogs.

10. The central boss from a shield of the second century BC dredged from the river Thames at Wandsworth. The design incorporates two birds with wings outstretched.

If Celtic Art reflects complex belief systems, then it could be argued that the distribution of items bearing Celtic Art must, to some degree, represent the area over which those belief systems were understood and probably practised. But the reality is more complex. Items of Celtic Art can be handed on in cycles of gift exchange until they are wholly removed from the context in which their meaning was known. A bronze bowl in Poland or a decorated sword scabbard in central Spain may mean nothing more than the passage of a valued item through exchange from one world to another. If, on the other hand, regional craft skills develop manufacturing the same or like items incorporating the same motifs or close local interpretations of them, then we may legitimately believe that something, at least, of the value system has been transferred.

As we have seen, the focal point of the early La Tène developments lay in the Marne–Moselle region and it was from here and probably also from Bohemia that the initial folk movements sprang. A study of the Celtic burials in the Po valley suggests that the different tribal groups still retained the burial traditions of their homelands. The Cenomani and Senones carried with them the traditions of the Marne region, while the Boii shared many characteristics with the burial practices evident in Bohemia. Here then the archaeological evidence is sufficient to suggest that the migrant populations carried much of their cultural baggage with them. Moreover, a study of early Celtic Art is now suggesting that immigrant craftsmen assimilated ideas from Graeco-Etruscan culture and fed them back northwards to further invigorate the Transalpine schools.

Moving further east, in Moravia, Transdanubia, the Tiza valley and Transylvania, cemeteries adopting classic La Tène characteristics are widely distributed. Swords are common and a lively school of craftsmen produced original designs for decorating the sword sheaths. While in the tradition of mainstream La Tène development, they are sufficiently distinctive to be designated the Hungarian Sword Style by art historians. In other artefact groups too there are also broad similarities across huge territories – the core zone and the eastern regions. In pottery for example a preference developed for elegant wheel-made jars decorated with impressed designs. While a number of regional styles are evident, what impresses are the broad similarities adopted from the Marne to Transylvania – communities spread across 1500 km are expressing a cultural preference.

It would be tedious to multiply the examples but taken together the archaeological evidence strongly suggests that the La Tène cultural package was accepted, adopted and maintained over a wide swathe of middle Europe. To what extent this was the result of large-scale folk movement it is difficult to say. That there was a flow of people from the early La Tène core region is reasonably certain but since the Danube valley was already well populated the probability is that the incomers were numerically in the minority. If so it is all the more notable that it was the incoming cultural package that became dominant. Some of the place-name evidence also suggests that the language spoken may have been Celtic. Thus while the population of a village in, say, central Romania may have had a very different genetic make-up from the population of the Moselle valley, they shared a similar material culture and presumably the values embedded within it.

The same cannot be said of the migrants who in 278 crossed the Bosphorus and Dardanelles to settle and raid in Asia Minor. Although, as we have seen, they retained the name Galatians, they seem soon to have abandoned all trace of La Tène material culture and instead embraced the culture of the region in which they found themselves. Whether or not their traditional belief systems were also given up it is difficult to say from the surviving evidence.

To the west of the early La Tène core zone, in western France, Britain, and Ireland, aspects of the La Tène cultural packages were differentially absorbed. In Armorica (modern Brittany), for example, which was recognized by the later Classical writers to be part of Celtica, the motifs of early La Tène Celtic Art were readily accepted and used to ornament pottery. The frequently illustrated urn from Saint-Pol-de-Léon in Finistère provides a spectacular example of this interaction. Inscribed on its surface is an intricate design of flowing palmettes and arabesques that have striking similarities to decorated metalwork found further east, pieces like a decorated disc from Auvers-sur-Oise or the Etruscan flagon intricately inscribed by a La Tène craftsman and now in the museum at Besançon in eastern France. There can be no doubt that the Armorican potter was fully aware of the decorative styles

11. Pot found at Saint-Pol-de-Léon, in Finistère (Brittany), dating to the fourth century BC. The design is based on motifs used by metalworkers.

current in the Marne region and beyond and wished to embrace them in his or her own art. The medium of transmission is most likely to have been decorated bronze vessels and other elite metalwork made in the central workshops and passed westwards, quite possibly along the Loire valley, through extensive exchange networks perhaps in return for tin and other raw materials. One such item, a finely decorated helmet, was found in the south-west of Finistère, and some of the Armorican pots closely copy bronze bowls of which the prototypes have not yet been found in the region.

As part of this same network of exchanges, knowledge of the metalworker's decorative art soon reached south-west Britain, Wales, and Ireland. A bronze hanging bowl or lid from Cerrig y Drudion in Wales was decorated in a style closely resembling the Besançon flagon though the technique was native British, and small bronze bowls of the type copied in pottery in Armorica are known from the south-west of Britain and from Ireland.

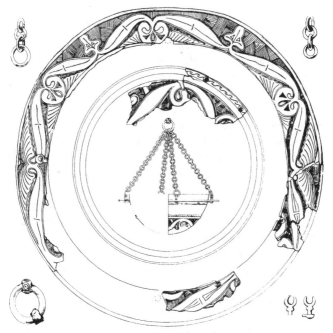

12. Bronze vessel from Cerrig y Drudion, Clwyd, Wales. It is thought to be a British-made piece, but the decoration is very similar to that on Breton pots.

Other routes besides the Atlantic seaways will have brought a knowledge of La Tène art to Britain. In the fourth or third century local craftsmen were making swords and scabbards in La Tène style and a little later a brilliant school of metalworkers somewhere in eastern Britain were producing highly original shields and the famous repoussé-decorated pony-cap found at Torrs in Scotland. It was not until perhaps as late as the second century BC that La Tène style elite metalwork began to be manufactured in Ireland. Thereafter the Irish smiths made an array of items all recognizably La Tène in style but showing modifications in form and decoration that are distinctively Irish.

The La Tène metalwork of Britain and Ireland must be seen against the background of developing indigenous culture. With the possible exception of a small incursion into eastern Yorkshire in the fifth century, there is no evidence at all to suggest the influx of an immigrant population. Local cultures continued to develop in an uninterrupted manner, long-established sites remained in occupation, and the native style of circular house was ubiquitous. That said, there is clear evidence that Britain, and to a lesser extent Ireland, remained part of an exchange network bound by sea routes to the Continent. It would have been via these systems that attributes of La Tène culture were transmitted to the islands, largely in the form of gifts, many of them exchanging hands among the elites. Besides manufactured goods like weapons and feasting gear, trained horses and their tackle, women with their personal and dress ornaments, and even skilled craftsmen may have been among the gifts. In this way large areas of Britain chose to adopt these outward and visible signs of La Tène culture as their own and came to accept the meanings and value systems that accompanied them.

The communities of Britain and Ireland were selective about the aspects of La Tène culture they chose to take over, but, viewing the spectacular array of fine metalwork produced in these islands, there can be little doubt that they became an integral part of the La Tène cultural zone.

Chapter 9
Gauls and Romans

'Gaul as a whole', wrote Julius Caesar in the opening paragraph of his *Commentaries* on the Gallic Wars, 'consists of three parts: one is inhabited by the Belgae, another by the Aquitani and the third by the people we call Gauls though in their own language they are called Celts. In language, customs and laws these three peoples are quite distinct.' Here, then, is what appears to be a useful generalizing statement about the ethnic structure of Gaul in the middle of the first century BC. Caesar goes on to give some geographical precision to the zones. The territory of the Celtic tribes is bounded on the south by the Garonne and on the north by the Seine and the Marne. To the west the Atlantic is the limit while to the north-east the Celts extend to the Rhine: further south the Rhône is the boundary.

Compared to the distribution of the La Tène culture of the third and second centuries, Caesar's Celts occupy a far more restricted territory, but this can, to some extent, be explained by the political and ethnic changes that had begun in the last decades of the second century.

In the south it was the Romans themselves who brought about the change. For the armies, and indeed the traders, who were active in the Iberian peninsula in the second century BC, the route leading from Italy along the north coast of the Mediterranean provided a vital line of communication. It passed through friendly territory controlled by Greek cities, like Massalia, but it was prone to attack from hill tribes living to the north. These attacks became so insistent that in 124 and 123 BC the Roman army was sent in to subdue the Ligurians, the Salluvii, and the Vocontii, and in 122 and 121 the Allobroges and Arverni along the Rhône valley were brought to heel. The newly won territory, together with that of the Greek coastal cities, was reorganized under Roman control to become the Province of Transalpine Gaul. Native settlements like Vienne and Geneva were taken over and the citizen colony of Narbo Martius was established near the old hill town of Narbo to control the route westwards via the Aude and the Carcassonne Gap to the Garonne and Gironde. A little later Roman power was extended to the Garonne with the establishment of a Roman garrison at Tolosa (Toulouse). By the time of Caesar's involvement in Gaul, the Romanizing process in the south was already sixty years old, the Provincia driving a wedge deep into the territory of the Celtic tribes.

In the north, too, dramatic changes were under way, though the details are far more obscure. As a broad generalization it would seem that the tribes of the north European zone, usually referred to as 'Germans' by the Classical authors, were pushing southwards into areas where previously La Tène culture had extended. One of the clearest cases of this was the settlement of a Germanic tribe, the Marcomanni, in Bohemia, the homeland of the Celtic Boii. Further to the west, Germanic tribes had crossed the Rhine and were beginning to establish new tribal homelands there. This great southward movement was under way by the last decades of the second century BC and it was well known to the Romans, who were ever fearful of ravaging hordes of barbarians from the north threatening Italy. In about 60 BC a Germanic tribe, the Suebi, led by Ariovistus, crossed the Upper Rhine with the intention of exploiting rivalries between the Sequani and Aedui – two Celtic tribes in north-eastern Gaul. At the same time the Helvetii, living in Switzerland, had decided to migrate *en masse* to the Atlantic coast, leaving their old homeland open to Germanic settlement. It was these events that provided Caesar with his excuse to march his legions into Free Gaul. Unless Rome took over Gaul, he said, the Germans would.

The region between the Seine–Marne and the Rhine was, according to Caesar, occupied by Belgae, who differed from the Celts. They were the toughest of all the inhabitants of Gaul, because they were furthest away from the enervating luxuries of the Mediterranean world and closest to the Germans, with whom they were constantly at war. Culturally, however, the southern part of the Belgic territory, as defined by Caesar, belonged to the La Tène cultural zone and is not easily distinguishable from that of the neighbouring Celts. Probably the simplest explanation is that the territory between the Seine and the Rhine shared a cultural gradient between Celtic La Tène and Germanic that was constantly being re-formed by tribal movements. At a level of simple generalization, it may be seen as a 'Celtic' territory undergoing progressive Germanization. At any event, Caesar, observing the situation first hand in the mid-first century BC, felt it necessary to differentiate the Belgae culturally and linguistically from the Celts.

The Gaulish tribes whom Caesar encountered were also a people in a state of transition. For more than three generations the tribes of the south and the east had been in close contact with the Roman world, and some of them, like the Aedui, had put themselves directly under Roman patronage. Several tribes were in the throes of dramatic social change, with the old warrior aristocracies, in which status was gauged by the number of followers a man could attract, giving way to a more stable form of government involving annually elected magistrates. Some, like the Aedui, had achieved this and had in place a rigorous system for strictly limiting the power of the magistrates, forbidding them to leave the tribal territory during their period of office, banning re-election, and restricting their families in applying for office. Any man attempting to return to the old system, who might 'aspire to kingship', faced the death penalty. One such unfortunate was Orgetorix of the Helvetii, who was the instigator of the tribe's planned migration. Accused of attempting to seize power, he evaded death by burning by calling upon his household and dependants to mass in a vast threatening horde. But later, after the magistrates had collected an army to support the rule of law, Orgetorix died, it was thought, by committing suicide. The incident reveals just how unstable the new form of government actually was.

The long period of direct contact with the Roman world provided ample opportunities for Roman entrepreneurs to set up lucrative trading networks with the tribes beyond the frontier. Cicero is quite explicit about this. 'All Gaul', he wrote, 'is filled with traders, is full of Roman citizens'. One of the commodities that was exported from northern Italy to Gaul in great quantities was wine. The Gauls' love of wine was described, with some relish, by Diodorus Siculus, quoting Poseidonius. Noting their tendency to drink themselves into a stupor, he goes on:

> For this reason many Italian merchants, with their usual lust for money, regard the Celtic passion for wine as a source of treasure. They transport the wine by boat on the navigable rivers and by cart through the open country and they get an incredibly good price for it: for one amphora of wine they get a slave – a servant in return for a drink!

In all probability there were enclaves of Italian traders ensconced in all the major tribal centres. This was certainly the case at Cenabum, the principal town of the Carnutes, when, in 52 BC, the native tribes of the Celtic zone rose against the Roman presence in Gaul. In the initial moment, Caesar tells us, 'They killed all the Roman citizens who had settled there as traders and plundered their property.' One of them was a Roman of equestrian rank who was organizing the supply of grain to the Roman army.

The course of events in the early years of the conquest suggests that Caesar regarded Celtic Gaul as virtually already subdued – subdued, that is, by the overlay of Romanization resulting from sixty years or so of contact with avaricious and enterprising traders. Having dealt, in the first year of the campaign, with the immediate problems posed by the migration of the Helvetii and the expansionist intentions of the German war leader Ariovistus, in 57 BC he turned his attention to the subjugation of the Belgae, and, having beaten a Belgic army at Bibax in the territory of the Remi, he quickly moved northwards against the more remote Belgic tribes, the Nervii and the Aduatuci. The Belgic engagement was under his personal command. Meanwhile his general Crassus was given the task of receiving the submission of the Celtic tribes of the Atlantic seaboard between the mouth of the Seine and the Loire estuary – the area he referred to as Armorica. After this the legions were established in winter quarters along the Loire.

The next season's campaigning was in all probability planned to be a great spectacular, with the army sailing across the Channel to demand homage from the British kings as well as a crossing of the Rhine – acts that, if successful, would have stunned the Roman populace with their daring. As it was, a rebellion broke out among the Armorican tribes led by the Veneti and plans had to be changed. The troops in winter quarters on the Loire were told to build boats, and, when the time for the spring campaign arrived, Caesar joined his army. Sending Brutus with the ships to attack the Veneti, who were known to be skilled sailors, Caesar moved against the tribe by land. The land campaign was indecisive but the great sea battle that eventually ensued in Quiberon Bay was a Roman victory and led to the Venetic capitulation. Caesar ends his description of events with chilling terseness: 'I decided that they must be punished with particular severity, so that in future Gauls would have a greater respect for the rights of envoys. I put all their elders to death and sold the rest into slavery.' Elsewhere in Armorica, in what is now Lower Normandy, Caesar's general Sabinus seems to have gained an easy victory – or so Caesar's description implies.

With the Armorican rebellion at an end, Caesar now had time for a late summer campaign against the coastal tribes of Belgica to prepare the ground for his delayed spectacular.

The next year, 55 BC, was to see him moving first across the Rhine to make a brief foray into German territory and then late in the summer, probably later than he had intended, crossing the Channel to make a precarious raid on the tribes of Kent. The following year he was back on the Channel coast making thorough preparations for a second invasion of Britain. This time he was more successful, bringing the powerful dynasts of Essex and Hertfordshire to submission. But on his return to Gaul, in the autumn, he found himself faced with a serious crisis in Belgica. Many of the tribes had taken arms against the Romans and, inspired by a charismatic war leader, had begun to get the upper hand. In the flurry of marching and countermarching which ensued a large Roman force with its two commanders was surrounded and annihilated but by decisive action Caesar managed to save the situation from disaster.

The next year, 53 BC, he decided to deal with the Belgae once and for all. It was a ruthless campaign during which huge numbers of the native population were slaughtered or sold into slavery and the countryside was devastated with fire and the sword in a deliberate policy of scorched earth: 'when we had laid waste the country in this way I withdrew the army.'

Early in the year Caesar had experienced a curious act of defiance from two of the Celtic tribes, the Senones and the Carnutes, who occupied territory between the Seine and the Loire. For the five years he had been campaigning in Gaul, this area, and indeed the whole of the central part of Celtic Gaul, had been quiet, but when, in the spring of 53, Caesar summoned the Council of the Gauls to meet, the Senones and Carnutes, together with the Belgic tribe the Treveri, refused to come. It was, he believed, 'the first step towards a war of rebellion'. A show of Roman military strength quickly brought them to heel, but the threat remained in the air and at the end of the campaigning season Caesar held an inquiry. The instigator of the conspiracy was executed and many others fled. It was the spark that set the whole of Celtic Gaul afire with rebellion.

What caused the Carnutes and Senones to defy Caesar we are never told, but it may be no coincidence that it was in the territory of the Carnutes that Druids, from all over Gaul, traditionally met together in annual assembly. The Druids held considerable power in society: moreover, they were the only true unifying force and for this reason were feared and hated by the Roman authorities. It may have been they who called the Gauls to stand against Caesar – we will never know, but the speculation is not unreasonable.

When Caesar returned to join his troops in Gaul in 52 BC he found the whole of the centre of the country in armed rebellion. The three powerful Celtic tribes, the Carnutes, Bituriges, and Arverni, forming a great arc from the Seine to the Garonne, were the backbone, but others soon joined, including even the Aedui, who had traditionally been ardent supporters of Rome. More worrying still, the insurgents were united under a single war leader, Vercingetorix. For Caesar it was a grim moment – his whole Gallic enterprise faced disaster.

In the event, by brilliant leadership, force of arms, and occasionally sheer luck, Caesar's forces succeeded in stamping out the rebellion in a long and brutal action, which culminated in the famous siege of Alesia – a hilltop settlement where Vercingetorix had allowed himself, together with a large number of rebels, to be shut in by the Roman army. The action culminated with a pitched battle between the Romans and a huge relieving force drawn from all parts of Gaul. If Caesar is to be believed, it numbered some 8,000 cavalry and 240,000 infantry: virtually every tribe from Celtic and Belgic Gaul was represented. Roman discipline once more prevailed. With the relieving force destroyed, it was only a matter of time before Vercingetorix and the others in Alesia surrendered. Although Caesar claimed that 'the whole of Gaul was now conquered', it took

Vercingetorix (d. 46 BC)

Towards the end of Caesar's Gallic Wars the Gaulish tribes
rose up in rebellion against Rome and in 52 BC Vercingetorix,
a member of the Arvernian aristocracy, assumed the role
of war leader. Vercingetorix was the son of Celtillus, who,
Caesar tells us, 'had once been the most powerful man in the
whole of Gaul and had been killed by his fellow tribesmen
because he wanted to become king'. In offering himself as
war leader, Vercingetorix appeared to be following his father
in aspiring to kingship. At first he was restrained by his
kinsmen and expelled from the town of Gergovia, but,
undeterred, he raised a force of dissidents and soon won over
his tribe, the Arverni. Other tribes then followed. His tactics
were to draw the Romans into battle, and throughout the
campaigning season major engagements were fought at the
oppida of Noviodunum, Avaricum, and Gergovia. It was at
Gergovia that Vercingetorix came within a hair's breadth of
beating the Romans, but Caesar just managed to pull off a
costly victory. Eventually, defeated in a field engagement,
Vercingetorix and his force retreated to the hill of Alesia,
where they were quickly encircled by the Romans. The hope
of Vercingetorix rested on the arrival of a vast Gaulish relieving force, but when the force arrived it was defeated by
the Romans within sight of Alesia. With no hope left, the
defenders of Alesia surrendered. Vercingetorix was taken
captive to Rome, where he languished in prison for six years
before being strangled at Caesar's triumph in 46 BC.

another campaigning season to deal with the many pockets of resistance that still remained.

Caesar and his armies had been actively campaigning in Gaul for eight years, each year slaughtering large numbers of people and enslaving tens of thousands of others. In many of the campaigns in northern Belgic territories, whole landscapes were torched. A contemporary estimate suggested that a million Gauls had been killed and another million sold into slavery. Out of a population of an estimated six or seven million, this was a devastating percentage. While the brunt fell on the Belgic tribes, the whole of Celtic Gaul had been caught up in the trauma. Every community would have borne the scars – resentment and recrimination must have rumbled on for generations.

Chapter 10
Britons and Romans

It is a well-known, and often repeated, fact that no Classical writer whose work survives ever referred to the inhabitants of Britain or Ireland as Celts. It could, of course, be argued that this observation alone cannot be taken to mean that they were not Celtic in some way, but the fact remains that the Classical authors perceived the inhabitants of the islands to differ in significant ways from those of Celtica in Gaul.

The whole question is neatly dismissed by Tacitus writing in the late first century AD. 'Who the first inhabitants of Britain were,' he wrote, 'whether natives or immigrants, remains obscure; one must remember we are dealing with barbarians'. Here, I suppose, we could leave the matter and pass on, but there are a few threads of evidence worth exploring further.

Julius Caesar, who had some first-hand knowledge of the south-east of Britain, offers a number of interesting insights. The population, he said, 'was extremely large and there were many farms closely resembling those of the Gauls'; and again, 'The most civilized of the Britons are those who live in Kent, which is entirely a maritime area; their way of life is very like that of the Gauls.' Elsewhere, when writing of the Druids, he offers the intriguing aside that it was generally thought that the Druidic doctrine developed first in Britain and was later introduced into Gaul: 'even today those who want to study the doctrine in greater detail usually go to Britain to learn there'. To Caesar, then, while the Britons and the Gauls were different peoples, their beliefs, values, and lifestyles were closely similar. Exactly the same point was made by Tacitus, who went so far as to suggest that 'the Britons were descended from Gauls who migrated to the island'. He goes on to support the hypothesis by noting that 'in both countries you will find the same ritual, the same religious beliefs. There is no great difference in language.' He then lapses into the old Celtic stereotypes: 'There is the same hardihood in challenging danger, the same cowardice in shirking it. But the Britons show more spirit: they have not yet been softened by protracted peace.'

The suggestion that people from Gaul had migrated to Britain was more explicitly made by Caesar, who contrasted the 'interior of Britain', where the people claimed to be indigenous, with the 'coastal areas', which had been settled by immigrant groups from Belgica. These he said still retained the names of the tribes from which they had originated. There is, indeed, some evidence from tribal names and from archaeology to suggest that people from northern Gaul might have moved into the Solent region and its hinterland in the early decades of the first century BC.

What the Classical world thought of Britain and Ireland before Caesar set foot in Kent is more difficult to discern, but there are a few threads embedded in earlier writing that are worth teasing out. In the fourth century AD a North African Roman, Avienus, wrote a pretentious poem called *Ora maritima* in which he spliced together his gleanings from a variety of earlier texts to give a fanciful account of the coasts from Massalia to the British Isles. One of the sources that he used, which could be as early as the sixth century BC but is more likely to be of the fourth century, describes the journey north from Armorica. 'There is a two-day journey for a ship to the Holy Island – as the ancients call it. The island is large in extent of land and lies between the waves. The race of the Hierni inhabits it far and wide. Again, the island of the Albiones lies near.' It is a muddled and difficult text to interpret and incorporates certain misunderstandings, but this aside it is generally agreed that the anonymous source tells us that at this early date Ireland was called *Hieriyo* and Britain *Albion*. Since both words appear to be an early form of Celtic, we may accept them to be the names used by the indigenous inhabitants.

It is quite possible that the source of this information was the book *On the Ocean* written by the Greek explorer Pytheas after his remarkable exploration of the Atlantic coasts of Europe in about 320 BC. Among his many achievements, Pytheas appears to have circumnavigated the British Isles, and the careful observations which he recorded of the land and its peoples in *On the Ocean* provided a source used by most of the later writers who chose to describe Britain, including Julius Caesar and the Elder Pliny.

Pliny, in writing of 'Britannia Island', tells us that 'Albion was its own name when all were called the Britannias'. He then goes on to list all the other islands including Isle of Man, Anglesey, Isle of Wight, the Orkneys, and so on. The implication is that the islands were collectively called the Britannias and that the largest, known to the Classical world as Britannia, was called Albion by its inhabitants.

One of the earliest surviving texts to use the Britannia name was written by the Greek geographer Diodorus Siculus and it is widely accepted that he was drawing heavily on Pytheas. The actual name used by Diodorus was *Pretannia*, which in the original source would have been *Prettanikē*. This would imply that the inhabitants were called *Pretani* or *Priteni*. The name survived as *Picts*, used by the Romans to describe the inhabitants of northern Britain beyond the frontier and in the Welsh for Britain – *Prydain*. That the word is generally believed to mean 'the tattooed folk' or 'the painted ones' raises interesting questions. It does not really sound like an ethnonym – the name used by a people to identify themselves – but more like a generalized description adopted by people to describe foreigners. If so, then it is possible that Pytheas learned it from the Celts of Armorica, who were describing for him their woad-painted neighbours across the Channel. Thereafter the inhabitants of Albion were called Pretani. By the first century BC the P had become B and the nickname given to the people of the island by the Gaulish Celts began to be used by Classical authors as the name of the island – Britannia.

Britain and Ireland were, throughout prehistory, locked into the complex network of exchanges that bound the Atlantic communities together and there is ample archaeological evidence to demonstrate this. There would have been preferred routes and ports of call changing with time, and the volume of traffic would have fluctuated, but as a broad generalization we can say that the communities facing Britain, from Finistère to the mouth of the Rhine, were probably in fairly regular contact with those on the adjacent coasts of Britain.

As early as the end of the fourth century Pytheas seems to have joined one such voyage from an unnamed Armorican port to the British port of Ictis somewhere along the south coast of Devon or Cornwall where the Britons brought tin for exchange. Later, in the early first century BC, there is convincing archaeological evidence for an active trade axis between the north coast of Armorica, possibly the bay of Saint Brieuc to Hengistbury Head overlooking Christchurch Harbour. It is quite possible that a small community of Armorican traders actually occupied the headland each year during the trading season. By Caesar's time the links between Armorica and Britain were still strong. Writing of the Veneti, he comments on their large number of ships and considerable sailing skills, saying that they regularly sail to and from Britain.

Further up the Channel there seem to have been long-established links between the Gaulish Belgae and the communities of south-eastern Britain. Gallo-Belgic coinage begins to find its way into Britain probably as early as the mid-second century BC. These high-value issues of gold would have been used in the gift exchanges that bound the elites of the two regions together in ties of friendship and obligation. Caesar makes an interesting reference to the Belgic ruler Diviciacus, king of the Suessiones, who, 'within living memory', had control not only over a large part of Belgic Gaul but also of Britain. This would seem to be suggesting that Diviciacus was a high king recognized as such by other rulers in Gaul and Britain. In some such social context it is easy to imagine gifts of gold being made in return for allegiance and perhaps for services.

Caesar's quick thrusts into the south-east of Britain briefly punctuated this long continuum of cross-Channel interaction, but, with the establishment of peace in Gaul under Roman rule, contact resumed and the pace quickened. It is quite probable that Roman traders now established themselves in the major native centres in the south-east.

The eventual conquest of Britain, initiated by the emperor Claudius in AD 43, can be seen as the inevitable culmination of these processes. The course of the Claudian conquest was determined very largely by the state of the different tribes encountered. In the south-east were two large confederations based around the Catuvellauni north of the Thames and the Atrebates to the south. These were the most thoroughly Romanized of all. Immediately beyond was an arc of less-developed tribes: the Durotriges, the Dobunni, and the Corieltauvi, stretching from the Dorset coast to the Humber estuary. These tribes issued their own coinage and had nucleated centres where power resided and trade took place. Beyond them in the west and north of the country were tribes with simpler socio-economic systems and more dispersed settlement patterns. All this would have been known to the Romans and provided the logic behind their initial invasion strategy: the civilized core was to be taken within the empire and the peripheral tribes speared through by the military frontier holding them firmly in place and confronting the undeveloped regions beyond, from which could be got metals, slaves, and other desirable commodities.

Within the civilized core, to ease the transference of power to the Roman state, two native rulers friendly to Rome were confirmed as client kings for the duration of their lives – Togidubnus in the Solent region and Prasutagus in East Anglia.

In the event the grand strategy had to be abandoned. The armies were soon drawn westwards into Wales and northwards, eventually penetrating deep into Scotland. By the early years of the second century the frontier was established along the Tyne–Solway line, though from time to time over the next century or so it was advanced to the Clyde–Forth front. A large part of what was to become Scotland, and the whole of Ireland, lay wholly beyond the frontier, though linked to the Roman province by trade, auxiliary service, and raid.

The picture of the Britain transmitted through the writings of Caesar and Tacitus conforms quite closely to the image of the Celt that they will have learnt through earlier historical writings. The British chariots particularly impressed Caesar. In one engagement his adversary Cassivellaunus commanded 4,000 chariots, which were used to devastating effect against the Romans. In Caesar's graphic description of the tactics of the warriors, the excitement of the writer is almost palpable:

Britons and Romans

> First they drive in all directions hurling spears. Generally they succeed in throwing the ranks of their opponents into confusion just with the terror caused by their galloping horses and the din of the wheels. They make their way through the squadrons of their own cavalry, then jump down from their chariots and fight on foot. Meanwhile the chariot-drivers withdraw a little way from the fighting positioning the chariots in such a way that if their masters are hard pressed by the enemy's numbers they have an easy retreat to their own lines.

After commenting on the skill and agility of the charioteers, he adds: 'I came to their rescue just in time for our men were unnerved

Boudica (d. AD 61)

Boudica was the wife of Prasutagus, king of the Iceni (a tribe occupying much of East Anglia), at the time of the Roman invasion of Britain in AD 43. Prasutagus, along with King Togidubnus of the Regni in central southern Britain, were allowed to retain their kingdoms as clients of the occupying Roman force for the duration of their lifetimes, after which the kingdoms were expected to be incorporated into the new province. In an attempt to circumvent this Prasutagus willed his kingdom jointly to the Emperor and his own daughters. This was unacceptable to the authorities and in a confrontation it is claimed that his wife Boudica was beaten and their daughters raped. This sparked a rebellion, with Boudica assuming the role of war leader. She chose her moment well, when the governor Sentonius Paulinus was campaigning in north-west Wales. Much of the south-east of Britain joined the revolt (but not, it seems, Togidubnus). Camulodunum (Colchester), Verulamium (St Albans), and London were attacked by the rebels, their buildings burnt and populations slaughtered. During this onslaught Boudica was accused of atrocities against her enemies. Eventually the Roman army confronted the rebel force in battle. Boudica still fought in the old way with charioteers to the fore and women on the baggage trains watching from behind. The Romans won a resounding victory, after which Boudica committed suicide by taking poison.

13. Celtic war chariot in action as depicted on the reverse of a Roman denarius minted in _c._48 BC.

by these tactics which were strange to them.' This statement, and indeed Caesar's long description of the chariot in action, suggest that he had not encountered this kind of warfare in Gaul, though among the Celts a century or more earlier it was well attested. In Britain, therefore, the archaic order of battle still persisted.

Chariots were to make their appearance again during Boudica's rebellion against the Romans in AD 60 and in the final battle of Mons Graupius, in which the general Agricola shattered the resistance of the Caledonian confederacy in the far north of Scotland in AD 83. In the aftermath of that battle Tacitus vividly describes the uncontrolled fury of the defeated Britons fluctuating between acts of great bravery and hopeless desperation. It is the old Celtic stereotype once more called upon to provide dramatic literary effect.

The Roman hold on Britain lasted for more than 350 years, but Romanization was patchy and confined largely to the south-east of the island. Towns and villas were restricted to this zone. Beyond lay Cornwall, much of Wales, most of the north above York, and, of course, Ireland. It was in these regions that the traditional ways of life, many of the old laws, the oral sagas, and the Celtic language survived.

Chapter 11
Interlude: the story so far

This is a convenient point to take stock – to examine the various strands of evidence that have been laid out in order to see if an entity distinctively Celtic can be drawn out of them or whether the whole cherished concept is an illusion.

First to recap. There are four broad categories of evidence that are relevant: the Classical sources; the archaeological evidence; language; and vernacular traditions. Each is different in quality and quantity and each has its own ground rules, which govern academic debate.

The Classical sources reflecting on the last half millennium BC gave the impression that Celts were everywhere in barbarian Europe, except where there were Scythians. The study of the language group that is called Celtic focuses on western Europe with a distinctly Atlantic bias, which, in part at least, is because it is only in the extreme west that the languages survive today. The vernacular literature is similarly restricted to the west, to Ireland and to a lesser extent Wales. The archaeological evidence, on the other hand, covers everywhere that human society lived and worked. For the prehistoric period it is largely anonymous, but, through the recurring patterns that can be discerned, it can inform at a number of levels, the most valuable, from our point of view, being the belief and value systems of societies and the degree by which, through exchange mechanisms, they were in contact with each other.

Each source of evidence has something to add to the debate, but what must be guarded against are circular arguments creating a compote of plausible compossibilities, such as – 'since philologists tell us this, the archaeological evidence can be interpreted thus: since archaeologists interpret their evidence thus, our linguistic suppositions must be correct'.

It is also necessary to be aware of the prejudiced mindsets that we bring to bear. In the days of rampant colonization in the eighteenth and nineteenth centuries, when the study of the Classical World dominated the education system, it was usual to think in terms of invasion and colonization as the sole begetters of change, more usually characterized as 'progress'. Lord Raglan could say without fear of contradiction that 'natives don't invent things'.

In the post-colonial, post-Classical era, the pendulum has swung to the other extreme and archaeologists have tended to downplay, or even totally reject, the idea of there ever having been invasions, basing their beliefs on the absence of archaeological evidence. This is too extreme a view. If one was relying entirely on archaeological evidence, it would have been impossible to discern the Celtic raid on Delphi or, for that matter, the settlement of Celts in Asia Minor. In so far as it is possible, we must keep our prejudices and preconceptions under strict control.

That said, there are, I think, two comfortable old myths that we can dispose of at the outset. The first is that there was a 'coming of the Celts' as expressed in the question 'When did the Celts first arrive in Britain?' All the evidence we have to hand shows that this is far, far too simplistic a view. The second is that there was such a thing as a pan-Celtic Europe – a kind of brotherhood of the Celts that would, at the time, have been recognized from one end of Europe to the other. This is the confection of politicians and popular writers.

So, what can be said? The evidence, so briefly sketched out in the previous chapters, allows us to offer a broad scenario by way of summary.

The development of the Celtic language is perhaps the most difficult question to tackle because of the extreme paucity of data from the pre-Roman period, but most philologists agree that early versions of Celtic were being spoken over much of western Europe by the sixth century BC from Iberia to Ireland to the Italian lakes. How far back in time a distinctive Celtic language could be discerned is a matter of pure guesswork and will ever remain so, but some observers are content to see its origins in the Neolithic period in the fifth millennium BC. There is nothing inherently implausible in this, and indeed the flow of ideas and beliefs that accompanied the development of settled agriculture would provide an appropriate context for the emergence of a language that would allow disparate communities to communicate.

Thereafter, as the archaeological evidence vividly demonstrates, the communities of western Europe shared many aspects of their continuously developing culture in common. The Atlantic seaways formed a major highway of communication, as did the great Atlantic-flowing rivers extending deep into Continental Europe, from the Rhine to the Guadalquivir. The networks of interaction apparent over the next 4,000 years or so would have provided conditions ideal for language development and convergence. By the Late Bronze Age (c.1300–800 BC) the entire zone was closely bound by exchange networks and was sharing knowledge of beliefs and technologies. This was the ambience in which the earliest known form of Celtic developed.

Over much of western Europe, including Britain, Ireland, and Iberia, the Late Bronze Age saw the emergence of a distinctive warrior-based society. Although there were considerable differences from one area to another, many values were shared in common. The accoutrements of the warrior – swords, spears, shields, and sometimes body armour – are plentiful in the archaeological record, as are the trappings of the feast such as cauldrons and roasting spits. This was also the time when hillforts began to be built in some number. The archaeology of the period is redolent with the evidence of a warrior aristocracy who indulged in hospitality as a central focus for maintaining group cohesion and fostering external relationships. It was not at all unlike the kind of society depicted in the works of Homer.

In the eighth and seventh centuries the same values and beliefs persist, but two zones of intensification and innovation can be discerned – a west central European zone, where the warrior aristocracy employs the horse and vehicle as a central part of the funerary ritual (this is Hallstatt C in archaeological terminology), and north-eastern Iberia, where a distinctive Celtiberian culture emerges. Both innovating centres are on the periphery of the Atlantic zone and may perhaps best be understood by seeing the areas between the Atlantic and Mediterranean systems as interface zones where precocious development is likely to happen. (Map, p. 31.)

All this is the immediate prelude to the barbarian world glimpsed by the Greeks. What they saw was a kaleidoscope of different cultures sharing a broadly similar language and a set of values that conditioned their behaviour. It was not unreasonable, therefore, for the Mediterranean observers to regard them as one people and to give them a name – the Celts – the name by which one of the communities they came into contact with identified themselves. Since the closest point of contact that the Greeks had with the northern barbarians in the sixth century was southern Gaul, in the hinterland of their colony Massalia, they may have coined the ethnonym used in this region. This was the region that Caesar, 500 years later, tells us was occupied by tribes calling themselves Celts. So it was that the concept of Celts as the peripheral barbarians first passed into history.

The late sixth century saw the introduction of a new dynamic that depended upon an interaction between the Mediterranean world and the barbarian periphery. The Hallstatt chiefdoms and to a lesser extent the Celtiberian chiefdoms were drawn into these interchanges, which in effect intensified the flow of raw materials from the resource-rich Atlantic zone to the consuming Mediterranean. In west central Europe the effect of all this was the emergence of a new elite zone – the early La Tène chiefdoms – which flourished in the fifth and fourth centuries, reinvigorating the ethos of a warrior society. (Map, p. 32.) This could well have been the context in which an oral tradition emerged embodying tales of raids, of chariot warfare, heroic single combat, and feasting – a tradition which, in a localized and much accreted version, miraculously survived as the Ulster Cycle in the Irish vernacular literature.

Along with the saga tales, other aspects of the belief system were shared over large areas. La Tène art, for example, was rapidly adopted and adapted in Armorica and Britain by the fourth century and in Ireland a century or two later. But it would be wrong to think of the entire La Tène cultural package emanating only from the core zone. Along the networks of interaction ideas would have flowed in all directions. Caesar's tantalizing statement, that Druidism arose in Britain, is a reminder of this (though we will never be able to test its validity).

It was probably in this period of intensive interaction, encompassing much of west central Europe and Britain, that the indigenous language of these regions developed the structure referred to as P-Celtic. Ireland, which lay outside the initial sphere of these influences (probably from the sixth to second centuries), retained its more archaic language form. The same was true of the Celtic-speaking communities of the Iberian peninsula, whose development no longer shared in that of west central Europe but became reoriented more directly to Mediterranean culture as the Phoenicians and Greeks took a stronger hold on the Mediterranean coastal zone.

It was from the core of the early La Tène zone and probably also from among some of the communities of eastern Gaul – the territory of the people that called themselves Celts – that migrants moved into the Po valley and along the Upper Danube into the Middle Danube valley and beyond. It is these Celtic migrations, seen through the distorting lens of Mediterranean scrutiny, that provide most of our common images of Celtic society. But by their very nature migrating people are likely to project a modified and selective image of their culture.

In the second and first centuries BC the dynamic changed again as the Celtic-speaking peoples came under increasing pressures from culturally different peoples around their border. From the Mediterranean, Roman influence spread relentlessly through Iberia and Gaul; from the north came the Germans, while in the east Dacian armies moved into the Middle Danube region, destroying the Celtic communities settled there. Eventually, by the end of the first century AD, one of these alien cultures – Rome – had swept through Europe to the Irish Sea and the Highlands of Scotland, meeting with the Germans and the Dacians along the Rhine–Danube axis.

Four centuries of Roman rule not only introduced a totally new set of cultural values, including the Latin language, but the very mobility of population within the empire will have mixed the gene pool, particularly in the frontier zones and in the cities. As traders and administrators moved in and retired foreign troops settled, newly recruited auxiliaries marched out to fight wars or patrol distant frontiers. So the genetic mix of the indigenous populations will have become more heterogeneous, its Celticness becoming diluted. Even so, people with Celtic names, occasionally writing in Celtic, were still throwing curse tablets into the sacred spring in Bath in the third or fourth century and the Celtic language was still to be heard spoken in countryside around Bordeaux. It is tempting to believe that the rural populations retained their native language in some form at least until the large-scale Germanic migrations of the late fourth and fifth centuries swept away the last traces of the old order except in the remote parts of the west – Armorica, Cornwall, Wales, northern Britain, and Ireland – where the Celtic language and some of the cultural attributes we call Celtic managed to survive.

This sketch of west European prehistory stresses the strong thread of cultural persistence running through it all, but it also emphasizes how complex are the problems if we try to reduce it all to simple (even naive) questions of ethnic identity. Perhaps we are trying to impose modern constructs of ethnicity on a time and place where they have little meaning. An inhabitant of Gaul in the third century BC would have known his lineage and his tribe and might even have known the tribes allied to them but little more. If a definition is demanded, we could either take the minimalist view and say that the ancient Celts were those whom Caesar said called themselves Celts – that is, tribes living between the Seine–Marne and the Garonne – or we could be more inclusive, accepting as Celts those who spoke the Atlantic European language we call Celtic. Since language has embedded within it shared values and beliefs and is often a cultural identifier, it may be preferable, if we feel the need of a definition, to accept the more all-embracing view.

Chapter 12

Threads of continuity: the Celtic twilight

The fifth century saw Europe descend into turmoil as barbarians from beyond the frontiers poured into the Roman provinces, disrupting, and in some places totally destroying, the infrastructure of Empire. In Gaul, Franks and Burgundians from what is now north-western Germany moved in to settle in the north, while Visigoths took over the south-west. To add to the confusion, contingents of Alans, Vandals, and Suevi swept through the country *en route* to Iberia and North Africa. Even more frightening was the horde of Huns who penetrated into north-eastern Gaul before being driven off by those who had already staked their claim. In Britain boatloads of different groups from the coasts of the Low Countries and Jutland – generally referred to as Anglo-Saxons – landed in the south-east of the country and quickly spread through Wessex and into the Midlands. Some of the same groups explored the Gaulish side of the Channel, eventually establishing their settlements in what is now Lower Normandy.

The exact numbers involved are difficult to assess and it may be that they have been overestimated in the past, but the overall effect was to erase the overlay of Romanization in the newly settled areas and to replace it with a very different culture. In these shattering upheavals the last vestiges of Celticness disappeared from view. This does not mean that the indigenous population was wiped out or displaced but simply that the remnants that survived were quickly subsumed within the alien culture.

Beyond the areas of Germanic settlement, in Armorica, south-western Britain, Wales, northern Britain, and Ireland, the native Celtic-speaking cultures remained largely unaffected. These areas were not, however, undisturbed, for it seems as though even the remote Atlantic-facing communities found themselves caught up in the frenzy of 'folk wandering' that now gripped Europe.

Raiders were active in the Irish Sea as early as the middle of the fourth century if not before, attracted, it would seem, by the plunder to be had in the coastal regions of what was then still the province of Roman Britain. In the 360s Scotti and Attacotti together with the Picts from beyond the northern frontier were active in plundering the northern part of the province. The Scotti at this time occupied the north-east of Ireland, while the Attacotti were either from the Western Isles or, more likely, also from Ireland. We know little of the events of this time but some of the raiders, both Scotti and Attacotti, later appear in Roman army lists serving on the Continent, in much the same way as 750 years before Celts had signed up as mercenaries in the service of the Greek tyrants.

The scale of the Irish raids on Britain is unknown, but St Patrick, who was captured in a raid in the early fifth century, writes of thousands of Britons being taken captive or killed at this time. One of the Irish kings, Niall of the Nine Hostages, is recorded in a poem to have led seven raids on the British coast, and one source claimed that his own mother was British, herself a victim of an earlier raid.

As well as raids there was also settlement. The Irish saga *The Expulsion of the Déisi* describes the migration of the tribe from Co. Meath across Ireland. Some settled in Munster and Leinster, while others continued on across the Irish Sea to find land in Dyfed in south-west Wales. Once established, the migrants maintained close

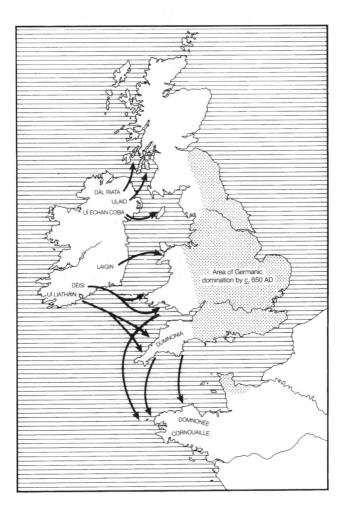

14. The movements of people between Ireland, Britain, and Armorica in the fourth to sixth centuries AD.

St Patrick (fifth century AD)

Uncertainty surrounds the dates of St Patrick. The Irish annals record his arrival in Ireland in AD 432 but give his death variously as 461 and 493 – a problem ingeniously explained by one scholar who suggested that there may have been two Patricks, but it is more likely one of the dates of his death, probably the later, is in error. In the *Confessio* written by Patrick in his old age the main outline of his story is recounted. As a youth he lived in a civilized part of Roman Britain, but he was captured by the Irish in a raid and carried off as a slave to a remote part of Ireland, where for six years he looked after the flocks and herds. One day he heard an angelic voice telling him his ship was ready which encouraged him to walk the 320 kilometres to the coast, where he found a ship, exporting hunting dogs, bound for Gaul. They reached the country in three days but found it devastated by barbarian raids and eventually Patrick managed to get back to Britain to join his family. However, heavenly voices encouraged him to go back to Ireland, this time as a missionary. Although there were Christian enclaves already established in the country, Patrick chose heathen and remote places for his mission and was evidently highly successful in attracting converts and setting up a Christian infrastructure. The system he adopted was based on the Roman system with administrative zones – like the Roman *civitates* – governed by bishops, but it did not fit well with the social system prevalent in Ireland and was soon replaced by monasticism.

relations with their kinfolk remaining in Ireland. The extent of the settlement, covering much of south-west Wales, is indicated by the distribution of stones carved with Ogam script. Another group of Irish settlers established themselves at about this time in the Lleyn peninsula of north-west Wales. Their origin is not immediately apparent, but in all probability they were Scotti. One Welsh tradition records that Irish settlers in the area were driven out by a force of Votandini from north of the old Roman frontier.

The north-eastern part of Ireland was, in the fifth century, inhabited by peoples known as the Scotti. The *Life of St Columba* records how a band of 150 of them, from Dál Riata in Antrim, sailed across the narrow North Channel to settle in Argyll some time at the end of the fifth or early in the sixth century, thus initiating the kingdom of Dálriada – a powerful polity that was to rule territories on both sides of the Channel for some time to come. That the Irish settlement in Scotland (as it can hereafter be called) was on a large scale is suggested by the distribution of Irish place names that extend through Argyll and Bute and down the Galloway peninsula. Much of western Scotland and the Islands was probably settled at this time; so too was the Isle of Man.

It has long been accepted by linguists that these fifth-century movements were responsible for the introduction of the Irish form of Celtic, which contributed significantly to Scottish Gaelic and Manx. While this may have been so, we should remember that these regions were physically close together and linked by the sea. The archaeological evidence clearly shows extensive contact and the sharing of culture going back to the Neolithic period. In such circumstances one might have expected the languages of the regions to have developed a high degree of similarity well before the mid-first millennium AD.

Some time about AD 540 a British monk – Gildas – wrote a book called *De excidio* bewailing the fate of the British population as they fled from the Anglo-Saxon settlers who had taken over much of south-eastern Britain and were thrusting westwards. In one particularly vivid passage he describes how the desperate Britons took to their boats and 'made for lands beyond the seas', singing as they went the psalm 'You have given us like sheep for eating and scattered us among the heathens'. It is generally assumed that they were sailing from the south coasts of Devon and Cornwall and were making for the Armorican peninsula. As early as 480 people in Armorica were being referred to as *Britanni* and by the mid-sixth century the peninsula was called Britannia (from which, of course, comes Brittany). At this time the Byzantine historian Procopius understood that communities from Britain were still arriving in Brittany, leaving their original homeland because of overpopulation.

There has been much debate about when people began to flee from Britain and what caused the migration. One view is that the outward movement may have begun as early as the late third century and was the direct effect of Irish attacks on the British coast, which may have continued intermittently throughout the fourth century, to be followed, in the fifth century, by the beginnings of Irish settlement in Cornwall. That the Severn estuary was a route of penetration for Irish raiders is well supported by archaeology, but there is no direct evidence of an Irish presence in Cornwall before the sixth century. That said, there is no reason why small groups of Britons should not have been sailing for Armorica throughout the troubled fourth century, presaging a more significant folk movement in the fifth and sixth centuries.

The immigrants seem to have settled in the north and west of the peninsula, where the Brytonnic place names Plou-, Tré-, and Lan- concentrate. These regions became known as Domnonée and Cornouaille, presumably taking the names of the British tribal territories from which the settlers came. As we have seen, there has been much debate about the impact of this migration on the emergence of the Breton language. All that needs be said here is that the long-held view – that Breton developed from the language of the immigrants – has given way to the acceptance that Celtic survived in Armorica throughout the Roman interlude to be invigorated by the settlers, whose language was anyway quite similar.

Sufficient will have been said to show that, during the fifth and sixth centuries, the Celtic-speaking peoples of the Atlantic zone, beyond the region settled by the Germanic immigrants, were in a state of considerable flux: there was much movement between them along the long-established sea routes. Over two centuries or so this resulted in a considerable displacement of population – it was as though the gene pool had been given a thorough stirring. What emerged was a distinctive Atlantic community bound more closely together by the realization that their language and traditions set them apart from the alien Anglo-Saxons and Franks who had amassed along their eastern borders: the Celtic-speakers now looked to each other.

During the time of the Roman Empire the Atlantic seaways, though still active, seem to have been of lesser importance to traders than the more convenient cross-Channel routes to northern Gaul, but with the demise of Roman centralizing power in the West, the Atlantic routes appeared reinvigorated. This is particularly well demonstrated by the finds of Mediterranean pottery, including amphorae, once containing oil and possibly wine from Asia Minor, Egypt, and North Africa, and fine red-slipped tableware from Asia Minor and North Africa, which are found scattered along the Atlantic coasts of Brittany, Cornwall, Wales, Ireland, and Scotland. Pottery of this kind reflects an active trading network in the fifth and sixth centuries, but how it was organized we can only speculate. Most likely the cargoes were carried on Mediterranean ships to the Atlantic ports of Iberia and from there were transferred to local vessels for the journey northwards. It is not unlikely that the cargoes were trans-shipped more than once, the last leg of the journey to Britain being in the hands of Gaulish merchants.

After the middle of the sixth century the supply of Mediterranean products seems to have dried up, but the Atlantic trading routes remained open throughout the seventh century, the cargoes now including a distinctive grey pottery made in western Gaul, in the Loire valley or further south in the Gironde region. Most of the vessels were jars, which presumably contained relishes of some kind, but there were some jugs among them, suggesting that the cargoes may also have included barrels of wine from the Bordeaux region. Like that of the earlier pots from the Mediterranean, the distribution of these seventh-century west Gaulish wares centred on the Celtic-speaking regions of the Atlantic, particularly around the Irish Sea and its approaches.

There are several historical texts that add further colour to the archaeological distribution maps. The *Life* of St Columba, who lived on Iona in the second half of the sixth century, mentions Gaulish seamen arriving from 'the provinces of the Gauls' in a *barca* – presumably a non-local type of ship. It is tempting to see them bringing the year's supply of wine and other foreign delicacies to brighten the existence of the monks. A century or so later we learn of a Gaulish bishop who ended up at Iona, having been shipwrecked somewhere in western Britain.

The foreign ships arriving in western Britain, no doubt, traded with the locals, taking back local products with them, and British shipmasters would have made the same journeys in reverse. The Irish ship on which St Patrick travelled in the early fifth century was trading in hunting dogs, presumably bred in Ireland, while in the seventh century we learn of Irish traders visiting the monastery on the island of Noirmoutier, just south of the Loire estuary, to trade their cargo of shoes and clothes.

These meagre scraps, gleaned from the few surviving texts and the distribution of discarded potsherds, are of immeasurable value in showing just how vital the Atlantic sea lanes were in the three centuries or so after the collapse of Roman authority. It was links

of this kind, threading the coastal waters, that bound the
Celtic-speaking coastal communities together: the rest of Europe
went a very separate way.

It was not just a mobility of people – raiders, migrants, and
traders – that gave these Atlantic communities their identity; over
and above this, it was a growing commitment to a distinctive belief
system – monastic Christianity – and the development of a series of
closely related art styles that served it.

Ireland was the innovating centre. Christianity was already
established here by the late fourth century. In 431 Palladius, a
deacon in the church in Gaul, was sent on a mission to the Christian
Irish. His presence made a limited impression in a small area of Co.
Wicklow, but the impact was to be far eclipsed by the activities of
Patrick, who the next year established a base at Armagh and from
there set out to minister and organize. The model he chose was the
parochia – a rural territory – with a church at its centre, the whole
system being placed under the authority of bishops.

The Patrician church was not to last, for a new idea – monasticism –
was beginning to spread. Originating among the Desert Fathers of
Egypt, it was quickly taken up in Gaul and spread to Brittany. From
there the new ideas were caught up in the currents that engulfed the
Celtic-speaking world. One of the earliest monastic establishments
in Ireland, founded on the island of Dair-inis in the estuary of the
river Blackwater, had close links to Brittany and with more distant
Mediterranean culture.

Monasticism spread quickly throughout Ireland, and by the end
of the sixth century the system set up by Patrick had all but
disappeared. Why this should have been is a complex issue, but in
part it can be explained by the social structure prevalent in the
west, in which families and kinship groups were strongly bonded.
Early Christianity required of its adherents penance and self-
mortification in the pursuit of salvation, and this could most easily

be achieved by removing oneself from the comfort of family to remote and deserted places. It was in this context that holy men – the saints of the Celtic church – began to journey outwards across the seas to found monastic establishments in distant lands: *peregrini*, they were called. Some, like Columba, crossed the North Channel to Dálriada and set up the community on the island of Iona. Others travelled much further. Samson spent his early life in the monastery on Caldy Island, off the south-west coast of Wales. From here he set out on a journey that took him via Cornwall to the north coast of Brittany, where he eventually founded a community at Dól, from which place he travelled widely in Gaul. By about AD 700 there were religious communities on the Faeroes and within a hundred years Irish monks had reached Iceland. Others travelled throughout Europe, founding monastic establishments in France, Germany, and Italy, wherever the opportunity presented itself.

15. **Aerial view of Christian hermitage, Church Island, Co. Kerry.**

The energy of the Insular faith was remarkable. So too was the religious art that accompanied it – sculptured high crosses, illuminated manuscripts, reliquaries, chalices, and a host of smaller items proclaim a great vitality. Evident in the designs are motifs derived from the La Tène heritage but integrated now with ideas emanating from Spain, France, and Germany to create something entirely original, and all for the glory of the Christian God. Irish Insular art and the British schools it inspired is one of the great artistic achievements of barbarian Europe comparable to La Tène art – its immediate predecessor in the west.

Sufficient will have been said to show that between the fifth and eighth centuries AD the Celtic-speaking communities of the Atlantic regions had emerged as a reasonably cohesive cultural entity. In language, religion, and art they shared a common heritage that distinguished them from the culture of surrounding polities. While there was, of course, much internal variation from region to region

16. **Silver chalice from Ardagh, Ireland, dating to the early eighth century** AD.

and hostilities often flared up setting communities against each other, it is the cultural unity that impresses – a unity that was in no small part dependent upon the mobility of the people blessed by having the sea as their principal means of communication.

Subsequent incursions of Norsemen in the eighth to tenth centuries and later of the Normans, English, and French into different parts of the Celtic-speaking regions did surprisingly little to dilute the native culture, which maintained itself in low profile while the rest of Europe did its best to tear itself apart in horrifying conflicts.

Chapter 13
Reinventing the Celts

While the disparate Celtic-speaking communities of the Atlantic seaways may, through the dim memory of shared histories and the reality of similar dialects, have recognized some degree of kinship, at no time did they consider themselves to be a nation nor can we find the slightest hint that they believed themselves to be Celts. For more than 1,000 years, following the collapse of the Roman world in the West, the concept of the Celts real or imagined seems to have passed out of consciousness.

Until the sixteenth century the emergent states of western Europe had been content to accept mythological stories of their origin and distant past – stories linked to the Bible or to the Trojan myth – but with the Renaissance came a desire to create a firmer base for history. Scholars such as John Leland (1503–52) toured the length and breadth of Britain at the time of the dissolution of the monasteries collecting manuscripts and making first-hand observations of antiquities. Elsewhere in Europe other scholars were discovering the writings of Classical authors tucked away in monastic libraries. Tacitus' *Agricola* had been published in Milan about 1480, while Caesar's *Gallic War* was made public in Venice in 1511. These and other ancient texts provided an entirely new framework for historians to work on. For the first time ancestors dating back to before the Romans could begin to be glimpsed.

Armed with an array of new sources, scholars could begin to write histories. In France Jean Le Fèvre published his *Les Fleurs et antiquités des Gaules* in 1532, while in England William Camden's *Britannia* was first published (in Latin) in 1586. For the first time visions of ancient Gauls and ancient Britons were being given some substance. It was, however, the Scottish historian George Buchanan who was to introduce the word 'Celt' into the discussion in his *Rerum scoticarum historia* published in 1582. Buchanan believed that the Celts originally lived in northern Italy, southern and central France, and western Iberia. In this he was presumably basing himself closely on Classical texts. From Iberia, he believed, the Celts migrated to Ireland, and subsequently some of them (as Scotti) settled in the west of Scotland. The inhabitants of the rest of Britain differed in that they were Galli who had migrated from Gaul. So it was that the Celts made their reappearance.

It was not until the end of the seventeenth and beginning of the eighteenth centuries that Celts were brought on to centre stage in the histories of France and Britain under the guidance of Paul-Yves Pezron (1639–1706), a Breton and one-time Cistercian monk, and Edward Lhuyd (1660–1709), a Welshman and Director of the Ashmolean Museum in Oxford. Both men had their own agendas – to gain proper recognition for the integrity of their countries at a time when the culture and identity of both were being threatened by neighbouring nation-states, respectively France and England.

In 1703 Pezron published his *L'Antiquité de la langue et de la nation des Celtes*. What he offered was, in reality, a new origin myth that provided the French in general, and the Bretons in particular, with grand and impressive genealogy. The Celts, he believed, arose in Asia Minor and spread to Greece and the rest of Europe in prehistoric times where they set up as overlords. From here they conquered Rome and Greece but eventually settled in western Gaul, their descendants surviving in Brittany and Wales, where the ancient language of the Celts was still spoken. It was a

Paul-Yves Pezron (1639–1706)

Paul-Yves Pezron was born in Hennebont in southern Brittany and educated first in the seminary at Rennes, later completing his studies in Paris. He was ordained and became a Cistercian monk, rising to become abbot of La Charmoye. But, tiring of administrative duties, he retired early to devote himself to scholarly study. His first book *L'Antiquité des temps rétablie* (1687) was concerned with world chronology after the Creation in 4004 BC, but more influential was *L'Antiquité de la langue et de la nation des Celtes*, published in Paris in 1703, in which he argues that the Gauls were *Celtae* and that they survived as Welsh and Bretons, who still spoke the language of the ancient Celts. He then attempted to give them a respectable pedigree by arguing that the Celts came from the east and were descended from Noah. They spread across Europe, conquering Romans and Greeks, and eventually ended up in Armorica (where, it will be remembered, he was born). In choosing to root the Celts, and by extension the Bretons and the Welsh, in the Book of Genesis, Pezron was giving them a more respectable ancestry than the Romans and British whose origins were linked to the Trojan genealogy. Pezron's work was known in Oxford to Lhuyd and his contemporaries, and in 1706 was published in English translation as *The Antiquities of Nations*. It remained influential throughout the eighteenth century.

straightforward story, resting, if somewhat lightly, on historical facts gleaned from the Classical sources and on philological observations of languages still spoken. More to the point it was a story which gave the Bretons an honourable ancestry as the direct descendants of the great warrior nation of ancient Europe.

For Edward Lhuyd, Pezron's book was an inspiration and one that gave direct support to his own ambition of establishing the antiquity of the Welsh, and it was he who encouraged the historian David Jones to translate it. The English version appeared in 1706 under the title of *The Antiquities of Nations, More particularly of the Celtae or Gauls, Taken to be Originally the same People as our Ancient Britains* – a significant modification of the original French.

Lhuyd had already embarked upon a comparative study of Welsh and Irish as early as 1692, and in 1694 he had met John Tollard in Oxford, who was engaged in studying Irish as a preparation for writing a book on the Druids. In the previous year Tollard had prepared a word list of Irish showing its similarities to Breton and this was presumably known to Lhuyd, who, by about 1698, was also getting news of Pezron's research. For Lhuyd, engaged in exhaustive fieldwork in Wales for his revision of the Welsh section of Camden's *Britannia* edited by Gibson and published in 1698, the last decade of the seventeenth century was a formative period during which his ideas about the identity of the 'Celts' were beginning to crystallize. He was a tireless researcher, visiting all of the Celtic-speaking countries of the west, with the possible exception of the Isle of Man, and corresponding widely.

His monumental *Archaeologia Britannica* was eventually published in 1707. In it he demonstrates the close relationship of 'the original languages of Britain and Ireland' and of Brittany, calling them collectively 'Celtic'. In the preface to the Welsh edition he began to sketch out his further thoughts, calling up a series of migratory movements to explain the various forms of Celtic then spoken. Buchanan's ideas of Iberian Celts settling in Ireland were tacitly accepted; so too were the ideas implicit in Pezron's work that Celts from Gaul settled in Britain. In this initial formulation lies the origin of the belief of two Celtic invasions of Britain and Ireland.

It is no mere coincidence that *Archaeologia Britannica* was published in the same year as the Treaty of Union was signed, which

Edward Lhuyd (1660–1709)

Edward Lhuyd was born at Glan Ffraid in South Wales of a Welsh-speaking family. He studied at St John's College, Oxford (1682–7) and became assistant to Robert Plot, first Keeper of the Ashmolean Museum, succeeding Plot as Keeper in 1691. As befitted his post, Lhuyd was a polymath with particular interests in natural history, fossils, stone implements, and British antiquities. He was recruited by Edmund Gibson to extend the Welsh section of William Camden's *Britannia* which he was editing. Lhuyd's contribution was substantial, incorporating highly accurate descriptions of monuments based on his own tireless fieldwork as well as considerations of material remains and folklore. After the publication of *Britannia* in 1695 Lhuyd focused his attention on a major project – the preparation for publication of the *Natural History and Antiquities of Wales* and an *Archaeologia Britannica*. To this end he travelled extensively between 1697 and 1701 visiting Cornwall, the Scottish Islands, Ireland, and Brittany. He made extensive use of questionnaires sent to correspondents and also collected original manuscripts (thirty-nine of which are in the library of Trinity College, Dublin). Finally, in 1707 the first volume of *Archaeologia Britannica* appeared – it was a *Glossography* in which he explored the affinities of Welsh/British and Irish, Scottish, Cornish, and Breton, which he considered to be Celtic languages. His failing health prevented him from producing further volumes and his copious notes were eventually largely dispersed.

united Scotland to England and Wales. For some while the morale of the Welsh had suffered in the face of creeping Anglicization, while the Union threatened the Scots with a similar fate. Lhuyd's book, in reaffirming the ethnicity of the Welsh and Scots and giving them a long and honourable pedigree, far more ancient than that of the English, instilled a new sense of pride and offered a firm intellectual basis upon which to recreate a distinctive identity. That both communities still spoke their own language was an added benefit, for henceforth language could be developed as the principal cultural identifier. The Welsh grasped the opportunity. In 1725 Sion Rhydderch published the first comprehensive Welsh grammar and for the rest of the century the popularity of the Welsh language steadily increased. Pezron's work had a similar effect in Brittany, but there the revival was short-lived.

The Treaty of Union was, in reality, the coming-together of Protestant interests in Britain to make a united stand against Catholicism and against the French. Given the mood of the time, it is easy to see why Lhuyd chose to call the language of the indigenous west Celtic rather than Gaulish – a name he might otherwise have considered adopting. In aligning his terminology with that of Pezron he was also joining the Welsh cause to that of the Bretons – both were minorities under threat of being absorbed by larger states.

One effect of the Treaty of Union was that the inhabitants of Great Britain not unreasonably began to refer to themselves as Britons – a word that had previously been used to identify the Welsh. Their name appropriated, it was not long before the Welsh were being referred to as Celts: the term was soon extended to embrace all those who spoke a Celtic language. Thus it may be said that the re-emergence of the Celts – some would say the reinvention – came about, in the early years of the eighteenth century, when political reaction to the development of nation states found support in erudite academic debate. Thereafter the concept of the Atlantic Celt past and present was taken up with enthusiasm and is still very much alive today across a wide spectrum of concerns from music to politics.

For the antiquarians and historians of the eighteenth century, Celts and Celticness quickly became a favourite theme. One of the most influential was William Stukeley (1687–1765), who, in 1723, began work on what was to be a four-volume *History of the Ancient Celts*. The project was never completed, but two volumes appeared, the first on Stonehenge in 1740 and the second on Avebury three years later. These monuments, Stukeley believed, were 'The temples of the Ancient Celts' and as such they were the preserve of the ancient priesthood of Druids. Stukeley's work began with meticulously observed drawings of the monuments and their landscapes, but, as Druidomania took hold, facts were modified to suit the ever-more fanciful theories. The plan of Avebury with its Avenue and the smaller circle known as the Sanctuary was gradually transformed until it became the plan of a serpent with a coil in its body (Avebury) and a head (the Sanctuary – which, conveniently, became more head-shaped in the later drawings). For Stukeley the works of the Druids were everywhere to be seen in the ancient monuments of the British countryside. Many others shared Stukeley's predilections. John Tollard, whose Irish word list was known to Lhuyd, wrote a *History of the Druids* in 1719, which was published in his collected papers in 1726 and 1747.

In Brittany Pezron's work also led to a new-found enthusiasm for Celts and Druids. *Les Celtomanes*, as they have been called, ascribed all the extant megalithic monuments to the period of the Celts and more particularly to the Druids. This belief pervades Malo Corret de la Tour-d'Auvergne's *Origines gauloises celles des plus anciens peuples de l'Europe* (1796) and Jacques Cambry's *Monuments celtiques* (1805).

While the excesses of the eighteenth-century antiquarians may seem amusing, even comic, now and it is easy to make fun of them, their theories and assumptions are part of the fascinating process by which archaeology has advanced. For them the megalithic monuments were without dates and it was not illogical to relate the greatest of the field monuments they were studying for the first time to their new-found concepts of the Celts. Not until the nineteenth century did a relative chronology based on the Three Age system – the concept of technological change from stone to bronze to iron – enable the antiquity of the megaliths to be gauged and separated from the age of the Celts. If, however, we accept the view, examined above, that the Celtic language originated much earlier, then perhaps the eighteenth-century scholars were not so wrong after all!

The Celtomania of the eighteenth century was to follow even more inventive courses. If the Scots, Welsh, and Bretons were the direct descendants of the Celts, could it not be, so the argument went, that in the culture of the present day it was possible to trace echoes from the past.

One of the first to have claimed to have done this was the Scot James Macpherson, who, between 1760 and 1763, published a series of poems ascribed to Ossian, son of Fingal, a semi-legendary Gaelic bard. The first volume was entitled *Fragments of Ancient Poetry, collected in the Highlands of Scotland, and translated from the Gaelic or Erse language*. Then followed two long poetical epics, *Fingal* (1761) and *Temora* (1763). His sources, he claimed, were two manuscripts 1200 or 1300 years old. If genuine it was an astonishing discovery and his work of translation was greeted with a rapturous enthusiasm. 'Ossian' was widely read and became a source of inspiration for freedom movements springing up in Europe in the early decades of the nineteenth century. Yet almost immediately it met with criticism and was castigated as a forgery. It is now generally believed that no such manuscripts existed and that Macpherson wrote the poems himself to provide Scotland with an epic tradition worthy of Homer, using his general knowledge of Gaelic oral tradition to give a sense of place and to add colour. That he may have had access to documents of the sixteenth century is also a possibility, but 'Ossian' as published is Macpherson's creation.

In Brittany, too, the search for the authentic voice of the past was soon under way. In 1838 a young Breton aristocrat Vicomte Hersart de La Villemarqué published a collection of ballads *Barzaz-Breiz* (*Songs of Brittany*), which he had gathered among the Breton peasantry. The work was an immediate success, since it provided exactly what the Celtophile romantics felt the need of, and others followed suit, scouring the countryside for old songs. As more became known and published, suspicion began to fall on the authenticity of *Barzaz-Breiz*, culminating in a scathing attack on La Villemarqué at the Interceltic Congress held at Saint-Brieuc in 1867. Particularly devastating was a publication by R. F. Le Men, timed to coincide with the conference, which directly challenged La Villemarqué: 'Play the bard, play the arch-bard or even the Druid, but do not attempt to falsify history with your inventions.'

After this La Villemarqué's credibility suffered, and it was not until the 1960s, when his original notebooks were discovered showing the full extent of the original works he had discovered and transcribed, that his reputation was to a large extent restored.

Le Men's cutting remark about playing the bard is a reference to La Villemarqué's visit to the Welsh Eisteddfod at Abergavenny in 1838, where he was made a bard. He records the event with wild enthusiasm in a letter to his father: 'I am a bard now, truly a bard! a "titled bard!" and I have been received according to the ancient rituals of the 5th and 6th centuries, handed down to our time.'

What he may not have realized was that the ceremony he attended was a confection of fantasy grafted onto some genuinely old traditions. The main part of the ceremony, known as the *Maen Gorsedd*, was an act invented in 1792 by a Welsh stonemason Edward Williams, otherwise known by his bardic name of Iolo Morganwy. It was pure theatre, rigid with ritual and dripping with

Hersart de La Villemarqué (1815–95)

Théodore-Claude-Henri Hersart de La Villemarqué was a Breton aristocrat who, at the age of 18, went to Paris to complete his studies. There, in the company of other ex-patriot Bretons, he developed a fervour for his homeland, writing emotional and mystical accounts of the countryside enhanced by transcriptions of Breton songs and pervaded by a thread of nationalism. By the age of 20 he was actively collecting Breton songs and searching for manuscripts as well as perfecting his knowledge of the Breton language. Enamoured by all things 'Celtic', he travelled to Wales in 1838 to attend the Eisteddfod at Abergavenny (where he was made a bard): he also visited Stonehenge and studied Welsh manuscripts in Oxford. On his return to Paris he tried to get official support for a proposed publication of Breton songs which he claimed closely reflected the stories and language of the sixth century bards. Support was refused, but *Barzaz-Breiz* was published at the author's expense in 1838. It soon became extremely influential not least in inspiring other folklorists to collect material of their own, and won La Villemarqué many academic honours. However, as more ballads were published it became evident that La Villemarqué's claims were exaggerated and at the Interceltic Congress held at Saint-Brieuc in 1867 he was publicly accused of forging evidence and misleading scholarship, and further criticism followed in the 1872 Congress from which he absented himself. In the 1960s La Villemarqué's original notebooks were discovered, throwing light on his methods of research and to some extent validating his claims.

symbolism, set against a backdrop of stone circles and Druidic altars. As a piece of pastiche it was Celtomania at its worst and still it continues today, obscuring the genuinely ancient traditions of the original ceremony.

The reinvention of the Celt at the beginning of the early eighteenth century came, as we have seen, at a timely moment. From it sprang a romanticism that pervaded antiquarian thought. The Celt was presented as a noble ancestor living in a heroic age: the Celtic-speaking communities, and to a lesser extent the English and French, were seen to be his successors. In the nineteenth century, as the discipline of archaeology matured and much of the old romantic accretion was stripped away, the Celt began to emerge as a symbol of the new nationalism that was beginning to awaken.

Chapter 14
Striving for identity

The froth of romanticism that followed the 'reinvention of the Celts' at the beginning of the eighteenth century was accompanied by rather more serious attempts to build identities and to create allegiances among the Atlantic communities who soon came to refer to themselves as the 'Celtic Nations' of Europe. Three threads can be distinguished all overlapping and interacting – cultural integrity, language, and nationalism.

To create cultural integrity it was necessary to set up institutions to identify and foster regional culture in all its various aspects and to perpetuate the results through regular publications and events. The Welsh were early on the scene with the foundation of the Society of Cymmrodorion in 1751 and the Society of Gwyneddigion in 1771, the latter devoted to the study of Welsh literature. Some years later the ancient tradition of annual bardic meetings, the Eisteddfodau, at which entertainers of various kinds – minstrels, songwriters, harpists, and satirists – came together to compete, was revived. In the middle of the seventeenth century the Eisteddfod was being written off as outdated, but in 1789, with the support of a group of London businessmen calling themselves the London Welsh Society, the idea was revived and the first modern Eisteddfod took place at Bala in north Wales. It was not long after this that Edward Williams created the theatrical pastiche Druidic ceremony – the *Maen Gorsedd* – which was grafted on to the Eisteddfod in 1819. The first national Eisteddfod was held at Llangollen in 1858 and the tradition continues, the pseudo-Druidic overtones remaining.

Perhaps a more significant event for Welsh culture was the creation of the Cambrian Archaeological Association in 1848, which brought (and still brings) together professional scholars and amateur enthusiasts alike intent on researching Welsh antiquity.

From an early date academic links were created between Wales and Brittany. It was at the Eisteddfod held in Abergavenny in 1838 that the Breton folklorist La Villemarqué was admitted to the bardic order and in 1870 the Cambrian Archaeological Association published an account of Iron Age cliff castles in Brittany contributed by R. F. Le Men (the vitriolic critic of La Villemarqué). More recently (1996–7) the doyenne of Breton archaeology P.-R. Giot has served as President of the Association.

In Scotland cultural development took a rather different route. The Jacobite rebellion of 1745 and its violent suppression, followed by the miseries of the Highland Clearances, devastated the traditional culture that had flourished in the more remote regions. The Highlander ceased to be perceived as a threat and as time passed his image became domesticated. Instrumental in this was the writing of Sir Walter Scott. In his romantic novel *Rob Roy*, published in 1818, the hero was based on the life of a cattle-raiding Highland thug. In a mere half century the wild and dangerous Gael was being repackaged for genteel consumption. Four years later, in 1822, George IV became the first English monarch to visit Scotland, dressed for the occasion in what was claimed to be authentic Highland dress – a tradition still perpetuated by the present Prince of Wales. Thereafter Scotland became increasingly acceptable as a tourist destination and with it came the need to project a distinctive cultural image. Genuinely ancient traditions of dress, communal gatherings, and recreations were nurtured, sanitized, and rechoreographed to become the kilt, Highland games, and Scottish dancing, now so beloved of American tourists. Yet alongside all the quaint reinvention there has been a long tradition of scholarship. One of the most revered institutions, the Society of Antiquaries of Scotland founded in 1780, continues to provide an important academic focus for Scottish studies.

In Ireland the Royal Irish Academy (still so-called), founded in 1785, provided the focus for Irish studies in a wide range of subjects including science, literature, antiquities, and history. The Society of Antiquaries of Ireland came into being in 1869 giving particular focus to the past.

Unlike Wales and Scotland, which have produced few literary figures of real international distinction, Ireland has been a powerhouse of creative writing. The foundation of the Gaelic League in 1893 provided an important stimulus. Its aims were wide – to keep alive the Irish language and to preserve Irish customs. Within a few years other institutions were set up. In 1899 Lady Gregory, W. B. Yeats, and others were instrumental in founding first the Irish Literary Theatre and later the Abbey Theatre in Dublin. The list of Irish writers benefiting, if indirectly, from this early flurry of enthusiasm for performance and the written word is impressive – Yeats, Synge, Shaw, Joyce, and Beckett. Lady Gregory's other great contribution to Irish studies was to publish a readable paraphrase of the stories of the Ulster Cycle, making the exploits of the early heroes available for the first time to a wide readership and reminding the world of the remarkable vernacular literature that Ireland had inherited. It is not too fanciful to see, in the biting satire of Swift, the landscapes of Synge and the epics of Joyce, something of this inheritance breaking through.

In France we find a more complex and sometimes ambivalent attitude to the Gaulish past. In the aftermath of the Revolution there was a deep-felt need to re-establish links with the past across the jagged divide that had opened up. In bringing to France the famous statue of the Dying Gaul, Napoleon was recognizing the power of the image in reminding his countrymen of their Celtic ancestry, and the foundation of the Académie Celtique in Paris in 1805 was intended to reinforce the message by encouraging scholarship and research.

The Celtic heritage theme was taken up again with some enthusiasm by his nephew Louis Napoleon, who was elected President of the Second Republic in 1848 and four years later engineered a coup that enabled him to assume the title of Emperor and with it the designation of Napoleon III. Thereafter, until his ignominious defeat by the Prussians at Sedan in 1870, he transformed French culture and values.

His early interest in Iron Age archaeology led him to sponsor a highly ambitious programme of fieldwork and excavation between 1860 and 1865 designed to provide the topographical and archaeological background of the campaigns of Julius Caesar. An Alsacian soldier, Colonel Stoffel, aided by up to 300 assistants, was given the task of tracing the sites of the main military engagements, including the famous last stand of the Celtic war leader Vercingetorix at Alesia, while J. G. Bulliot excavated the capital of the Aedui at Bibracte (Mont Beuvray). Both projects were promptly published, the former as the magisterial *Histoire de Jules César* with Napoleon III as its author. Meanwhile the large collection of Iron Age artefacts that Napoleon's various activities had amassed formed the basis of Le Musée Nationale des Antiquités established in Paris in 1863.

It is impossible now to disentangle Napoleon's motives for engaging in these remarkable projects. No doubt he had a real academic interest in the past, but he would not have been oblivious of the power of the past to influence the present. France was under threat from an external aggressor – the Germans, hitherto disparate states who were fast aspiring to nationhood. The Gauls too had been under threat from the Germans when Caesar invaded – but there was the awkward fact that the Gauls had been defeated by the Romans. The valiant defence of their land was a matter for national pride, but then, so too was the fact that the Gauls settled down in peace with the Romans (French archaeologists have always referred to the culture of Roman Gaul as 'Gallo-Roman') and together they held the Germanic menace at bay, enjoying 400 years of prosperity. It was a complex message to get across and one not without its ambiguities.

Even today archaeology is still sometimes called to the service of politics. In 1984 President François Mitterrand initiated a new campaign of excavations at Mont Beuvray financed by the French state. The work was carried out by multinational teams under overall French control and led to the creation of the *Centre européen d'archeologie du Mont Beuvray*. It is not unreasonable to suggest that this institution should be seen against the background of French championship of the European Union.

But there are other ambiguities in the French claim to their Celtic past. The large-scale influx of Franks, Burgundians, and Visigoths into Gaul in the fifth century, greatly diluting the indigenous gene pool, was seized on by the Bretons, whose land was not settled, to support their claim that they were the only true descendants of the Celts. As early as 1843 the Association Bretonne was set up, but a more serious claim was made with the establishment of the first Interceltic Congress held at Saint-Brieuc in 1867. In issuing a call to kith and kin in all the other 'Celtic Nations' – Cornwall, Ireland, Wales, and Scotland – to send delegates, La Villemarqué was challenging the French establishment's hijacking, as he saw it, of Celtic archaeology. It is not insignificant that the first Interceltic Congress was called only two years after the emotional erection of the colossal statue of Vercingetorix at Alesia by the French. This was the time when the French state was actively suppressing Breton culture and language.

In Brittany a number of scholars were busy reinforcing Breton culture by researching oral tradition, particularly that preserved in the ballads. La Villemarqué's early work of *Barzaz-Breiz* was followed by collections by other folklorists, notably François-Marie

17. Statue of the Gaulish war leader Vercingetorix erected under the authority of Emperor Napoleon III in 1865 on the site of Alesia, where Vercingetorix made his last stand against the Romans in 52 BC.

Luzel (1821–95); Jean-Marie de Penguern (1807–56), and Anatole Le Braz (1859–1926).

A rather more romantic and wide-ranging view of the Celts was contained in Ernest Renan's influential essay *The Poetry of the Celtic Races*, published in Paris in 1854, in which he developed the concept of a structural opposition between Celts and the other races of Europe. In the very opening paragraph Renan contrasts his native province of Brittany with adjacent Maine and Normandy. As you enter Brittany, he writes,

> a cold wind arises full of vague sadness and carries the soul to other thoughts; the tree-tops are bare and twisted; the heath with its monotony of tint stretches away in the distance; at every step the granite protrudes from soil too scanty to cover it; a sea that is almost always sombre girdles the horizon with eternal moaning.

For him this symbolizes the dour inner nature of the Celtic Breton in contrast 'to Norman vulgarity, to a plump and prosperous population . . . '. This opposition he sees in all other regions of the Celtic west.

As an aside, it is worth noting that Renan's essay had a deep impact on Matthew Arnold and considerably influenced his O'Donnell lectures given in Oxford in 1865–6, entitled the *Study of Celtic Literature*. In the last of these he called for the establishment at Oxford of a Chair of Celtic. The first Professor of Celtic took up his appointment in 1877. Oxford was not renowned for the speed of its decisions.

The remoteness of Brittany, evoked by Renan, was a source of attraction to others. 'La vie sauvage' that Brittany personified drew artists to its coasts every summer and the Pont Aven community of painters, graced by Paul Gauguin until the call of the *sauvage* led him to Tahiti, became world famous not least among Americans. By the end of the century the remoteness had become quaint and fascination with the 'otherness' of the countryside and its people had become nostalgia expressed in many thousands of postcard vignettes generated for visitors and even in the titles of the best-selling books of folklore by Anatole Le Braz – *In the Land of Pardons*, *Tales of Sun and Mist*, and *Old Stories from Brittany*. Le Braz was all too conscious that Brittany was degenerating into what we would now call a theme park. In 1901 he wrote:

> you take several openwork steeples, a few calvaries, a tune from the *biniou*, a couple of notes of *bombarde* (highly recommended, the *bombarde*!); you add a sprig of broom, a bouquet of gorse, some wind, mist, rain and sea; mix it all up, shake vigorously . . . and you have Brittany.

The creation of cultural identities in the Celtic-speaking countries has, understandably, depended upon nurturing languages. But minority languages have a natural tendency to die out. This is true of the Celtic languages. The last Cornish speaker died in 1777. Manx is no longer spoken except on certain ceremonial occasions and the others are under threat in spite of a growing desire to nurture them.

Most successful has been Welsh. Empowered by the Welsh Language Act of 1967, which directs that Welsh has equal validity with English in the Principality, the language has grown in strength and now has the highest number of habitual speakers of any Celtic language. Compulsory Welsh is taught in all schools and one school recently even went so far as to require its pupils to sign an agreement not to speak English anywhere on school premises (a highly dubious demand surely contrary to Human Rights). Ireland, where the government gives considerable sums in economic aid to Gaelic-speaking areas (Gaelachts), now has the largest number of Gaelic speakers (over one million), but barely a fifth are habitual speakers. In Scotland Scottish Gaelic is still widely spoken in the Hebrides and the desire to maintain it as a living language is strong, but elsewhere in Scotland Gaelic speaking is in a steady decline. In

Brittany, in spite of strenuous efforts to maintain the language, the devastating damage caused by the French official desire for homogenization in the nineteenth century means that the decline has not yet been halted and many think it is too late to do so.

Yet there are some sparks of hope. Revised Cornish – an academically constructed language based on what survives from the past patched up with Welsh and Breton – is spoken by a handful of enthusiasts and has recently (2002) been recognized as one of Britain's six official minority languages, giving it recognition under the European Charter for Regional or Minority Languages. In Cornwall road signs are now appearing in Cornish and the first Cornish language film *Hwerow Hweg* (*Bitter Sweet*) has already been released.

In 1532 Brittany was ceded to France. Across the Channel union has taken longer. The Treaty of Union of 1707 brought England, Wales, and Scotland together, but it was not until 1 January 1801 that the United Kingdom of Great Britain and Ireland came into being. Union has inevitably brought with it calls for independence, which became increasingly loud and strident during the twentieth century, and all four of the Celtic-speaking countries have seen groups of extremists prepared to use terror tactics.

In Ireland matters finally came to a head in the general election of 1918, when Sinn Fein – the political party seeking Irish independence – won 73 of the 105 Irish seats but, instead of sending its representatives to Westminster, set up its own Republican government in Dublin – Dail Eireann – whose first act was to call for the 'evacuation of our country by the English garrison', encouraging its military wing, the Irish Republican Army, to engage in guerrilla warfare. Eventually in 1921, after long negotiations, the Irish Free State was set up in the south, soon to become Eire, leaving the six counties of the largely Protestant north as part of the United Kingdom. The Civil Rights movement of the early 1960s and the sectarian violence that flared up in 1969 have led to a long period of bloodshed and recrimination in Northern Ireland. The Good Friday Agreement of 1998 may yet provide a way forward. Meanwhile it is an interesting reflection that in Ireland the divide caused by religion appears to override the call for unity.

In Wales and Scotland the move towards regional independence has been more sedate and only rarely troubled by serious violence. The various small nationalist groups of the nineteenth and early twentieth centuries eventually gave way to the Welsh Nationalist Party (Plaid Cymru) established in 1925 and the Scottish National Party in 1934, but local interest in independence was slow to develop. In the referenda on limited autonomy held in 1979 the Welsh overwhelmingly rejected the offer while only about a third of the Scottish voters were in favour. By 1998, however, attitudes had changed and in that year a wide range of powers were devolved to the Scottish Parliament and the Welsh Assembly. How much further devolution will go remains to be seen.

In Brittany opposition to French centralism finally began to organize itself with the Union Régionalist Bretonne founded in 1898 and thereafter there have been a number of groups demanding separation from France but usually with comparatively little serious support. During the Second World War the Parti National Breton, founded in 1932, put forward a plan to negotiate independence after the defeat of France by the Nazis in 1940. The plan came to nothing but the suggestion tarred Breton nationalism with the brush of Fascism. More recently the cause of independence has been taken up by a left wing, environmentalist movement *Emgann* (Combat) who campaign on a wide range of local issues. Occasionally there are acts of violence like the bombing of a McDonald's restaurant in 2000 by a group calling itself the Armée Révolutionnaire Breton (ARB), but for the most part, while the Bretons enjoy a comparatively high standard of living, the debate focuses around green issues and the need to nurture Breton language and culture.

18. An independence rally in Brittany.

Meanwhile, while each of the Celtic-speaking countries has its own organizations pursuing local concerns, the spirit of the old Interceltic Congress is kept alive. In 2001 the Congress met in Rennes under the theme 'History in the Celtic Countries Nowadays – People without memory are a people with no future'. One of the sites visited was the battlefield at Saint-Aubin-du-Cormier, where, in 1488, the Bretons fought for their independence – and lost.

Chapter 15

Every night a *fest noz*: the new Celtomania

Brittany, more than any of the other Celtic-speaking countries, rejoices in its past. Drive through the countryside in July or August and everywhere you will see invitations to *fest nozou* and *fêtes folkloriques* – most of them 'traditional' events started in the last twenty or thirty years to provide a secular counterbalance to the far more ancient religious ceremonies called *pardons* held annually on saints' days.

'La nuit de la saucisse', held every July in the town square of Plestin in the Côtes-d'Armor, is a fairly typical example of a *fest noz* of the more elaborate kind. The main events are musical but there is plenty of food to be had from stalls around the square – *moules et frites*, *crêpes*, and of course *saucisses*, as well as wine and cider. The music varies from year to year but always involves traditional Breton music – the music of the biniou and bombarde – and group dancing. Everyone, old and young, locals and visitors, takes part. This is interspersed with the performances from invited musicians. The contrast between the offerings can sometimes be surprising. One year an impressive state-of-the-art coach drew up and a troupe of elegant young Galician dancers and musicians dressed in black and white traditional dress got out to give a display of Galician dancing choreographed with spectacular precision. Their act was followed by a group of English Morris men who had arrived on the ferry at Roscoff and cycled the 35 kilometres to the party evidently having discovered the delights of the local cider on the way. The incongruity was of no importance – everyone was there to participate and to enjoy the traditions, genuine or invented, that others brought to the event.

Two weeks later the commune of Ploulec'h staged their *fête folklorique*. Some years it is held in the bourg of Ploulec'h, other years on the promontory of Le Yaudet overlooking the sea at the mouth of the river Léguer. All the roads are closed, car parks are organized, and visitors are charged for admission. The event falls into two parts. The afternoon is strictly folkloric: village life a hundred years ago is re-enacted. Women wearing the *coiffe* and Breton costume scrub clothes at a specially constructed pond. A peasant, *sabots* stuffed with straw, grinds turnips in an ancient machine while a blacksmith shoes a patient, and much-shoed, carthorse. Some years a lethal-looking threshing machine with threatening belt-drives clangs and fumes away and just occasionally there is the guest appearance of a mole-catcher, who proudly explains a macabre exhibition of his craft resplendent, naturally, in his moleskin waistcoat. Streets are lined with very ancient farm machinery and in odd corners granite-cutters and sabot-makers ply their crafts.

Although the prime aim of the operation is to make money for the commune (which is carefully apportioned to a variety of works from sheltered homes for the elderly to new sports facilities for the young), the event provides entertainment for tourists and is greatly enjoyed by those who take part.

In the evening a large part of the local community joins in with a communal meal served in the open air on long trestle tables. There is an improvised dance floor and a microphone and events are allowed to take their own course, with the audience actively participating. Breton folk dancing is interspersed with singing and, rarely, with recitations of long-remembered poems. To hear Breton intoned to the ocean as the evening fades and the sea darkens is unforgettable. In hushed intensity the entire audience becomes one with itself and with its past.

It is all too easy to write off the *fest nozou* and *fêtes folkloriques* as modern inventions designed to entertain the tourists. They are much more than that. They provide the way by which the community can grasp hold of its past and relish a deep sense of being with ancestors and with place. In Brittany modern times have been short. The residents of Ploulec'h do not need to hire fancy dress if they still have the clothes of their parents or grandparents, and the farmer who provides the antiquated farm gear for exhibition may have been using it until the 1960s: the past does not have to be reinvented but simply called to mind. And so it is in many of the remote parts of Atlantic Europe.

Music continues to play an important part in Breton life, not only as a means of enjoyment but also as a symbol of a shared Atlantic culture. Several towns now host international music festivals. One of the earliest to be promoted was the Bagpipes Festival that took place in Brest from 1953 to 1970. It has since been eclipsed by the Lorient Interceltic Festival held in August each year and regularly attracting over half a million visitors. Needless to say groups from all the Celtic-speaking regions perform to audiences that, while predominantly Breton, are truly international. Other towns, like Quimper, are now following suit.

The popularity of these events has provided a real stimulus for the development of new music and the emergence of composer-performers of real talent. At the more popular end Alan Stivell has become almost a popular hero, while more classical music is represented by the work of the pianist Didier Squiben, who incorporates the rhythms and cadences of traditional Breton music and of the sea into his strikingly original compositions. Both Stivell and Squiben are artists creating something quite new out of themes from the local past and contemporary influences from the wider world. In this they are behaving as the potter who in the fourth century BC created the decorated jar from Saint Pol-de-Léon.

Let us stay with Brittany to explore some other themes of continuity and reinvention.

Death was in the forefront of the Breton consciousness. Many churches contain stark visual reminders of its ever-presence to engage the attention of their congregations – the Dance of Death painted around the walls of the chapel of Kermaria-an-Iskuit, and the Ankou, the grim reaper with his scythe, threatening the worshippers at Ploumilliau. But perhaps the most dramatic statement of the importance of death and ancestors to the rural population is in the account given by Charles Le Goffic in the late nineteenth century of the rituals associated with the disposal of the dead he observed at Trégastel on the north coast of Brittany. Here bodies were buried in individual graves and left for six or seven years for the flesh to rot and then were dug up and the bones stacked in an ossuary, or charnel-house, which occupied one corner of the churchyard enclosure. After many years, when the ossuary was full, the last stage in the long-drawn-out disposal process was enacted.

When Le Goffic arrived on one Saturday evening he found that a large pit had been dug and two large linen sheets had been placed just outside the porch of the ossuary. Inside 'were a little girl and a boy of twelve years up to their armpits in the mouldy fragments; they were cleaning the bones and passing them to a troop of little fellow-workers of both sexes, who received them reverently in their aprons, and carried them to one or other of the sheets'. Children were chosen to transfer the relics because the task could only be performed by the innocent.

Throughout the night the heaps of bones were protected by a circle of lighted candles and next morning before first light a Mass was said for the dead. Then at 4 a.m. the procession set out from the church.

> The parish cross went first, then came the clergy, the celebrant immediately after the cross, all in funeral vestments. The officiant stooped at the shroud and took up a skull, raised it aloft, and this was the token that the translation was inaugurated. Every one of the clergy and assistants followed suit, each took up a bone, even the four choristers in red, who stooped and gathered bones as they sang, and the crowd streamed after, every member of the procession carrying bones.
>
> I shall never forget the scene that ensued. Each of the faithful signed himself on the brow, on the eyes, and on the mouth with the bone that he had selected. It was a grey autumnal morning, and the candles of the choir burnt like phosphorescent points of light. The procession moved twice round the churchyard, and then halted at the pit. There the officiant placed the first bone in it and all followed in silence, bowing themselves and gently lowering the fragments, after kissing them, into the hole.

It is, of course, impossible to say how ancient was the ritual performed by the people of Trégastel just over 100 years ago, but it is tempting to speculate that it may have been very ancient. Their distant ancestors who built the megalithic tombs 4,500 years before would have found the proceedings far less surprising than we do today.

Acknowledging the memory of the dead is still a matter of importance in Brittany. Its focus is the ceremony of Toussaint (All Saints) held on 1 November. In preparation the churchyards are cleaned by volunteers working with the municipality and the individual graves are flooded by a sea of chrysanthemums. In the Christian calendar Toussaint follows the ceremony of All Souls, 31 October–1 November, when the souls of the dead are said to revisit the realm of the living. In the pre-Christian world this was the ceremony of Samhain, centring on the liminal period between the end of one year and the beginning of the next. Liminal interludes were dangerous. They were times when anything could happen and it was only by careful adherence to ritual and propitiation that a precarious order could be maintained. In Irish mythology it is the period when divinities and the spirits of the dead move from the underworld among the living and sometimes interfere, with devastating effect, in human affairs.

It is this same concept and package of beliefs that comes down to us today in the rituals surrounding Halloween. In the last two decades of the twentieth century, Halloween saw something of a revival in western Europe, largely as the result of a reintroduction of an Americanized version in a form attractive to young children. In Brittany today, towards the end of October, it is customary to see some shops and newspaper advertisements encouraging us to buy flowers for ancestral graves for Toussaint, while others tempt with the merchandise of Halloween – pumpkins, witches' hats, and the like. Few people realize that both events spring from the same pre-Christian ceremony of Samhain: they have developed their very different identities through many stages of reinvention. Tradition is persistent but may manifest itself in divergent ways.

The folk culture and folk traditions of the Celtic-speaking countries are very varied and have been recorded assiduously. They form a rich resource for those who wish to enhance, to recreate, or to invent identities. We have chosen in this section to focus on Brittany. The other Celtic-speaking regions could provide examples of equal richness and fascination, but in Brittany, more perhaps than anywhere else, the disjunction caused by the modern world has been less destructive of true continuity. One of the effects of this is that its Bretonness, far from being backward looking, is taking on a highly creative and innovative stance – here identity is progressive rather than retrospective.

Chapter 16
So, who were the Celts?

For many people in the world, not only in Europe but in America, Australia, and South Africa, the Celts are an emotive subject. Like the American who wrote to me about his alcoholism, the idea of being a Celt provides a raft of emotional support – a sense of being rooted back in a heroic past and an explanation of behaviour. How many times do you hear 'it's in my Celtic ancestry'? Attempt to take away that support and it will generate a reaction of puzzled hurt, as Simon James found after the publication of his *The Atlantic Celts: Ancient People or Modern Invention*. At one level, then, the concept of Celt is a belief, however mistily understood, that underpins sense of self and of inheritance. Archaeologists who wish to deconstruct that belief for strictly academic reasons should reflect on the need that, through time, humans have had to define their identity – a need that requires the constant restatement and reinterpretation of the many symbols of their perceived ethnicity. The concept of Celt is ever evolving.

In this last chapter, therefore, let us review the multifarious Celts who have peopled our world, our beliefs and our imaginations.

To the early Greeks – historians/geographers like Hecataeus and Herodotus – the Celts were the barbarians of western Europe, extending from the Atlantic coasts of Iberia and Gaul to the source of the Danube. This understanding was, in all probability, based on actual information provided by the Greek colonial enclaves that clustered around the shores of the north-west Mediterranean – cities like Massalia (Marseilles), Agathe Tyche (Agde), and Emporion (Ampurias) – founded around 600 BC. Knowledge of the Celts will have been derived from direct contact between the Greek settlers and the indigenous inhabitants and possibly from travellers who explored the interior. By the end of the fourth century BC the Massaliot adventurer Pytheas notes that the land of the Celts (Keltícē) extended northwards to the Channel. Centuries later Caesar confirms this geography.

At this stage, then, the Celts (people who called themselves Celts) occupied central and western Gaul, while others, known as Celtiberians, were to be found in central and western Iberia. Although the material culture of these two regions differed, they spoke similar languages and it was presumably for this reason that the early Greek writers had no difficulty with the generalizing concept that they were all Celtic. There is also some evidence to suggest that closely similar languages were probably being spoken in Ireland and Britain as early as the fifth century.

From the fourth century onwards the Graeco-Roman world came into direct contact with migrating bands of northern barbarians, whom they called variously Keltoi, Celtae, Galli, Galatae. For the most part these peoples were settlers, raiders and mercenaries and there was a belief that they originated in the 'Celtic' area of Gaul, though archaeology would suggest that the homeland of the migrant bands probably spread over a broader zone stretching as far east as Bohemia. Familiarity with this barbarian mêlée led to the development of a generalized stereotype of 'the Celt' as a warrior barbarian redolent of a distinctive pattern of beliefs and behaviour.

To some degree archaeological evidence supports the idea of a broad cultural similarity between these Celtic groups. Many of them shared in the cultural package that archaeologists have designated La Tène, a fact that, at the very least, implies the acceptance of a common system of behaviour and belief, though it may have been variously reinterpreted by disparate groups. To the Graeco-Roman world, then, the mobile, warlike, peoples of western and central Europe were an ethnic group – the Celts – who could be characterized and caricatured as the barbarians from without. By the late second century BC, after the threat of Celtic attack had subsided, the image subtly changed to that of the 'noble savage' as seen through the eyes of Poseidonius, who has been called, with some reason, a soft primitivist.

The Classical writers, then, present a gradually changing view of the Celts. To begin with (sixth–fifth centuries) they were simply dwellers in north-western and western Europe. Later (fourth–second centuries) they were barbarian savages – a threat to civilization. Finally (second–first centuries), the image mellowed and they took on more the aspect of anthropological other – a focus of scholarly interest.

The archaeological, and to some extent the philological, evidence presents a complementary picture. In the *longue durée*, the Atlantic zone of Europe from southern Iberia to the Shetland Isles was a region bound by networks of interaction greatly facilitated by the sea. This ocean-facing zone was tied back into Europe by a series of major rivers that, over the millennia, provided corridors of communication. It is not at all unreasonable to see the Celtic languages (as first defined in the eighteenth century) as evolving gradually in this Atlantic zone and converging some time around 1000 BC, when Atlantic exchange was intense, as a series of mutually understandable dialects spoken in the coastal and island zone and its riverine hinterland. It would have been this linguistic region that the Classical writers identified by the name Celtic, after one of the tribes known to them who spoke the language.

In the fifth century a group of elites – the early La Tène culture – emerged within the Celtic-speaking zone. From this core region a belief and value system, most readily visible in what is generally called 'Celtic Art', spread into the Atlantic zone, Britain, and later into Ireland. It may well be that as part of this package a particular dialect of Celtic – known as P-Celtic – was also transmitted, though probably not as far as Ireland. While it used to be conventional to consider the mechanism of this spread as one of migration and invasion, there is no convincing archaeological evidence to suggest that this was so, and indeed much to support the idea of the continuity of indigenous cultures in these regions. Nowadays archaeologists have no difficulty with the concept that change may be spread through networks of interaction by elite emulation – that is, the acceptance of 'foreign' ideas and styles by indigenous leaders to enhance their own status.

The situation to the south and east of the early La Tène elite zone was different. Here the archaeological evidence would support the view that large-scale folk movement inspired, at least in the first instance, by the migration of Celtic-speaking groups, impinged on Italy, the Balkans, and Anatolia. The 'Celticity' of these groups would have been very different from that of the communities of Atlantic Gaul and Britain and, indeed, from that of the Celtic-speakers of Iberia, who were largely unaffected by the early La Tène cultural package.

Is it legitimate to call this broad range of disparate communities Celts? It would be less misleading to refer to them as Celtic-speakers and to restrict the term Celts to the peoples of central and western Gaul, whom the early Greek historians, Pytheas, Poseidonius, and Caesar regarded, unambiguously, as Celts.

Those Celtic-speaking areas that came under the control of Rome gradually adopted new identities and a new language, and the indigenous gene pool will undoubtedly have become diluted with Mediterranean, east European, African, and Near Eastern genes introduced by traders, soldiers, and administrators. Though Celtic was still being spoken by some in Britain and Gaul in the fourth century AD the homogenizing effect of Romanization is likely to have blurred memories of ancestry and created new visions of ethnicity. The subsequent migrations of north Europeans into these areas, culminating in the Viking/Norman episodes, further intensified the dynamic of change. After the seventh century AD most of the population of Gaul and much of that of Britain can no longer be regarded as the inheritors of the Celtic-speakers of prehistory.

But the same is not true of the remote regions of the west. In Armorica, south-west Britain, Wales, Scotland, and Ireland indigenous Celtic-speaking populations remained largely unaffected by the disruptive events of the first eight centuries of the first millennium AD. They retained their languages and to a great extent their indigenous cultures. The sea remained the principal mode of communication between them, and from the third until the seventh centuries movements of populations between the Celtic-speaking areas served to intensify the cultural identity of the remote regions of the Atlantic zone, which became the focus of a remarkable cultural upsurge largely inspired by their distinctive interpretation of Christianity. There is an interesting comparison to be made between the elite-led artistic development of La Tène art and the church-inspired artistic flowering of early Christian Ireland. In both cases the artistry is symbolic of a complex of beliefs and behaviour embedded within the society and in both it was transmitted beyond its centre of development.

To what extent the inhabitants of these separate regions regarded themselves as part of a single ethnic group it is difficult to say nor is there any indication that they thought of themselves as Celtic: it was, no doubt, their tribal affiliation that provided the most immediate sense of identity. Yet, that said, the early Christian Celtic-speaking communities of the west were the direct successors of the pagan prehistoric Celtic-speakers of the same region. In using phrases like 'Celtic Christianity' or 'the Celtic West' archaeologists and historians are not being entirely outrageous.

The vision of the Celt, called into being in the eighteenth century

carn

A LINK BETWEEN THE CELTIC NATIONS

No. 116   **Winter 2001/02**   € 4.00 ⟩ Stg£2.50

40th YEAR SPECIAL ISSUE

Alba

Éire

Mannin

Cymru

Kernow

Breizh

CELTIC MUSIC FLOURISHING

CELTIC LANGUAGES IN EDUCATION

CELTIC STICK GAMES

INTER-CELTIC LINKS

ON THE POLITICAL FRONT

ALBA: COMANN CEILTEACH • **BREIZH:** KEVRE KELTIEK • **CYMRU:** UNDEB CELTAIDD • **ÉIRE:** CONRADH CEILTEACH • **KERNOW:** KESUNYANS KELTEK • **MANNIN:** COMMEEYS CELTIAGH

CELTIC LEAGUE ⊛

19. *Carn* – a publication dedicated to forwarding the cause of the 'Celtic' communities of the west.

and refined and remodelled to suit the growing nationalism of the nineteenth century, is undoubtedly encumbered with a great deal of modern baggage, much of it dredged up and sanitized from the murk of folk traditions or simply invented for the purpose of giving a sense of pedigree to political aspirations. Yet in stereotyping themselves the neo-Celts are simply redefining an identity already securely rooted in the largely indigenous nature of their inheritance and in the remarkable survival of their language. They are doing no more than the Greek and Roman writers who, more than 2,000 years before, were providing an identity for the barbarians on their northern borders, the more easily to engage with their foreignness.

The concept of the Celts is an ancient one that has changed with time: the Celts are always being reinvented, sometimes by outside observers, sometimes by the people themselves. If we were to take a tough purist line we might be prepared to admit that present-day Bretons could claim to be descendants of Celts, in that Caesar said that the inhabitants of central and western Gaul called themselves Celts, that their language and culture probably survived the Roman interlude, and that there has been comparatively little population change since then. No other region qualifies on all three counts. But many would find this definition unnecessarily restrictive, arguing instead that all those regions where Celtic languages are regularly spoken today may claim some relationship to Celtic roots in the prehistoric period. This does *not* mean that they were descended from Hallstatt aristocracies or La Tène elites but that they are the inheritors of an Atlantic culture and language that is far more ancient.

Further reading

There are, as one might expect for so popular a subject, a huge number of books on the Celts. In offering some suggestions on further reading I have, of necessity, been very selective, limiting myself to no more than four titles under each broad heading. I have chosen works published in English each offering a lengthy bibliography which, if thoroughly persued, would provide a lifetime of entertainment. I have omitted all those, however attractively produced, that rely on tertiary sources and have little themselves to add. Needless to say the 'lunatic fringe' has no place here!

The European prehistoric background

B. Cunliffe (ed.), *The Oxford Illustrated History of Prehistoric Europe* (Oxford: Oxford University Press, 1994).

—— *Facing the Ocean: The Atlantic and its Peoples* (Oxford: Oxford University Press, 2001).

K. Kristiansen, *Europe before History* (Cambridge: Cambridge University Press, 1998).

General books on the Celts

B. Cunliffe, *The Ancient Celts* (Oxford: Oxford University Press, 1997).

M. J. Green (ed.), *The Celtic World* (London: Routledge, 1995).

J. Haywood, *The Historical Atlas of the Celtic World* (London: Thames and Hudson, 2001).

S. Moscati (ed.), *The Celts* (Milan: Bompiani, 1991).

Celts through the eyes of the Greeks and Romans

H. D. Rankin, *Celts and the Classical World* (London: Croom Helm, 1987).

Celtic Art

R. Megaw and V. Megaw, *Celtic Art from its Beginnings to the Book of Kells* (2nd edn., London: Thames and Hudson, 2001).

I. M. Stead, *Celtic Art* (London: British Museum, 1985).

Religion

J. L. Brunaux, *The Celtic Gauls: Gods, Rites and Sanctuaries* (London: Seaby, 1988).

M. Green, *The Gods of the Celts* (Gloucester: Alan Sutton, 1968).

S. Piggott, *The Druids* (London: Thames and Hudson, 1968).

M.-L. Sjoestedt, *Gods and Heroes of the Celts* (Dublin: Four Courts Press, 1994).

Insular vernacular literature

M. Dillon, *Early Irish Literature* (Chicago: University of Chicago Press, 1948).

H. J. Jackson, *The Oldest Irish Tradition: A Window on the Iron Age* (Cambridge: Cambridge University Press, 1964).

T. Kinsella (trans.), *The Táin* (Oxford: Oxford University Press, 1969).

J. T. Koch (ed.), *The Celtic Heroic Age* (Malden, MA: Celtic Studies Publications, 1994).

Language

P. Russell, *An Introduction to the Celtic Languages* (London: Longmans, 1995).

Modern Celts: a myth?

M. Chapman, *The Celts. The Construction of a Myth* (New York: St Martin's Press, 1992).

S. James, *The Atlantic Celts: Ancient People or Modern Invention* (London: British Museum Press, 1999).

Some further references: works mentioned in the text

S. Baring Gould, *A Book of Brittany* (London: Methuen & Co., 1901).

J. R. Collis, 'Los Celtas en Europa', in M. Almagro-Gorbea and G. Ruiz Zapatero (eds.), *Los Celtas: Hispania y Europa* (Madrid: Actas, 1993), 63–76.

—— 'States without centres? The Middle La Tène Period in Temperate Europe', in B. Arnold and D. B. Gibson (eds.), *Celtic Chiefdom, Celtic State: The Evolution of Complex Social Systems* (Cambridge: Cambridge University Press, 1995), 75–80.

M.-A. Constantine, *Breton Ballads* (Aberystwyth: University of Wales Press, 1996).

J. H. Delargy, *The Gaelic Story-Teller: With Some Notes on Gaelic Folk-Tales* (Reprints in Irish Studies 6; London: Cumberlege, 1945).

D. E. Evans, 'The Early Celts: The Evidence of Language', in M. J. Green (ed.), *The Celtic World* (London: Routledge, 1995), 8–20.

—— 'Linguistics and Celtic Ethnogenesis', in R. Black, W. Gillies, and R. Ó Maolalaigh (eds.), *Celtic Connections*, i. *Language, Literature, History, Culture* (East Linton: Tuckwell, 1999), 1–18.

D. Prigent, 'The Lorient Interceltic Festival', *Carn*, 115 (2001), 8.

P. Sims-Williams, 'Celtomania and Celtoscepticism', *Cambrian Medieval Celtic Studies*, 36 (1998), 1–35.

J. R. R. Tolkien, 'On English and Welsh', in H. Lewis (ed.), *Angles and Britons: O'Donnell Lectures* (Cardiff: University of Wales Press, 1963).

Further reading

Index

Index

Expand your collection of
VERY SHORT INTRODUCTIONS

Visit the
VERY SHORT INTRODUCTIONS
Web site

www.oup.co.uk/vsi

- ➤ **Information** about all published titles

- ➤ News of **forthcoming books**

- ➤ **Extracts** from the books, including titles not yet published

- ➤ **Reviews** and views

- ➤ **Links** to other **web sites** and main OUP web page

- ➤ Information about **VSIs in translation**

- ➤ **Contact** the editors

- ➤ **Order** other **VSIs** on-line

CLASSICS
A Very Short Introduction
Mary Beard and John Henderson

This Very Short Introduction to Classics links a
haunting temple on a lonely mountainside to the glory
of ancient Greece and the grandeur of Rome, and to
Classics within modern culture – from Jefferson and
Byron to Asterix and Ben-Hur.

'The authors show us that Classics is a "modern" and
sexy subject. They succeed brilliantly in this regard …
nobody could fail to be informed and entertained – and
the accent of the book is provocative and stimulating.'

John Godwin, *Times Literary Supplement*

'Statues and slavery, temples and tragedies, museum,
marbles, and mythology – this provocative guide to the
Classics demysties   its varied subject-matter while
seducing the reader with the obvious enthusiasm and
pleasure which mark its writing.'

Edith Hall

www.oup.co.uk/vsi/classics

ARCHAEOLOGY
A Very Short Introduction
Paul Bahn

This entertaining Very Short Introduction reflects the enduring popularity of archaeology – a subject which appeals as a pastime, career, and academic discipline, encompasses the whole globe, and surveys 2.5 million years. From deserts to jungles, from deep caves to mountain tops, from pebble tools to satellite photographs, from excavation to abstract theory, archaeology interacts with nearly every other discipline in its attempts to reconstruct the past.

'very lively indeed and remarkably perceptive … a quite brilliant and level-headed look at the curious world of archaeology'

Barry Cunliffe, University of Oxford

'It is often said that well-written books are rare in archaeology, but this is a model of good writing for a general audience. The book is full of jokes, but its serious message – that archaeology can be a rich and fascinating subject – it gets across with more panache than any other book I know.'

Simon Denison, editor of *British Archaeology*

www.oup.co.uk/vsi/archaeology